Scripts & Strategies In Hypnotherapy

By

Roger P Allen, Dp. Hyp.PsyV

Published by The Anglo-American Book Company,
Bancyfelin, Carmarthen, Wales.

First published in the UK by

The Anglo-American Book Company Limited
Crown Buildings
Bancyfelin
Carmarthen
Wales

First published 1997.

British Library of Cataloguing-in-Publication Data
A catalogue entry for this book is available
from the British Library.

ISBN 189983608X

Printed and bound in Wales by
WBC Book Manufacturers,
Waterton Industrial Estate,
Bridgend, Mid Glamorgan.

Dedication

I dedicate this work to my wife, Jill, with thanks
for love and understanding beyond measure.

Table of Contents

Acknowledgements

I find myself wishing fervently that I could remember each and every source of inspiration used within these pages. I have gleaned so much from the talks and seminars which I have attended, videos I have watched, tapes I have listened to, and, of course, from general conversations with others in the profession. I have no intention of making any claim to the many concepts in this book, or to indulge in any pretence that the ideas used in these scripts are anything other than an amalgamation of the products of many people's efforts which have become part of universal knowledge now.

The following is an honest attempt on my part to give credit where credit is due, and perhaps even to acknowledge that much of what I might call my own is but my own interpretation of ideas and thoughts coupled with experience shaped and coloured by the input of others before me - those whose influences have become a part of my therapeutic aim of helping those who come to us seeking help.

I have certainly been influenced by the late great master, Dr. Milton H. Erickson M.D., as, I would suggest, have so many before me. A special mention must be made of Bandler and Grinder, Steve and Connirae Andreas, Havers and Walters, Citrenbaum, King and Cohen, all of whom have figured greatly in my reading.

My approach in general within the book has been to give specific credit when I have been sure of the source. If I do not accurately record a source of inspiration, I would hope to be forgiven; my intention is honourable.

To all of those who have helped me with suggestions for scripts and with so much material, I express my heartfelt thanks and feel sure that those who will use the contents of this book will do so fully within the spirit in which it was submitted.

To Michael Carr-Jones and Tony Powell, I give special thanks for their unfailing positivity and encouragement.

Foreword

I expect that in most cases you, the reader, will be a new and beginning hypnotherapist. I remember well those very early days, when I sat nervously awaiting my very first paying client. On the wall hung my newly acquired diploma, and how conscious I was of the date upon that piece of paper! I had purposely hung it in a position where it could not be seen by clients other than when they first walked through the door. When sitting in my therapy chair, it was well situated within the far limits of peripheral vision.

My first client was a smoker, and, when he walked into the office, I noticed immediately that he was extremely nervous. I hoped that I was succeeding in my attempt to appear the confident professional, and that he would not pick up on the fact that I was quietly terrified.

The session went extremely well. After asking the relevant questions to discover his motivations and fears, his values and what was important to him, I then asked him to make himself comfortable and proceeded to induce hypnosis.

I used a script for smoking cessation that had been supplied by my teacher and mentor, Michael Carr-Jones, and, at the end of the session, I collected my first fee. I heard some months later that my first client was still not smoking, this information relayed to me from a client referred to me by him.

As time has allowed me to grow more confident in what I do, I have begun to realise that, although much therapeutic intervention is derived from the reactions of our own subconscious response to the client, the value of scripted material is important as it provides the framework for so many of my sessions.

Much of what I use is material which I have read in magazines and books, ideas picked up from seminars and simply ideas from the work of other therapists. I take these ideas and write them down so that now I have a database of scripted material and strategies that I can refer to whenever I am planning a therapy session.

It has been established in various schools that students who are using scripts in induction procedures invariably achieve better results. To begin with, the use of a script to induce hypnosis may appear somewhat constrictive, rather like building up a model from a pre-formed kit of parts. No imagination is needed: you just follow instructions and at the end you have your model airplane or whatever. In time you will develop a "feel" for the manner in which the scripts are structured and, as your confidence grows, you will venture beyond the framework and begin to add to it from your own unconscious resources.

You will find, for example, that the framework of the script which I have provided for smoking cessation can be modified for many other habit problems, as the verbiage becomes for you the tools of your trade that you can use in whatever way is effective and appropriate. As a developing hypnotherapist, you will evolve for yourself a style that you are comfortable with, as you move forward from within the guidelines that allow you to take those first tentative steps to becoming the effective therapist that you aim to be.

I make no apology for the fact that the scripts I have provided here will in some cases prove very similar to others that you may acquire from other sources. The reason I include them is that they meet the need, and in all respects the work that I have done in writing scripts for myself has to be recognized as an amalgamation of ideas. I will of course claim, and trust that you, the reader, will accept, that much of the material has incorporated within it a great deal of myself and my own responses to the problems that I have encountered.

This book is the product of many hours of dedicated and detailed work. It also includes the thoughts and ideas of a multitude of people, all utilized by me to construct what for me has been an invaluable basis for the therapy work that I so much enjoy.

It is for you to determine the value of my efforts, and I trust that the contents of this book will serve you well. Your comments, suggestions and questions are cordially invited, as you will no doubt make your contribution to the wealth of ideas that ensure that this great profession moves ever forward.

Roger P. Allen
Hampshire, UK
March 1997

Introduction

By way of introducing this work which contains much of that which is necessary to begin therapeutic practice utilising the medium of hypnosis, I feel that it is necessary to define in broad terms the elements that will be covered.

So much has been written concerning the "state" that is termed hypnosis and the attempts to describe it in scientific terms have been many. For the purposes of this book, I would describe the "state" of hypnosis as an altered "state" of awareness that will allow access to the subconscious, having reduced the critical analytical interference of the conscious rationalising processes.

The process of inducing hypnosis is in effect a focusing of the conscious processes to a point where an altered "state" of awareness is achieved. In this "state", those activities can be relaxed to the point where we still "hear", as our normal physical abilities are not impaired. This is similar to being engrossed in a television programme, whilst overhearing a conversation in the background.

Basically, all else just fades into unimportance. "There are three main components of the process of inducing hypnosis: relaxation, imagination, and enactment." **Hildegard & LeBaron, 1984**

The subconscious part of the mind continues to hear all that is to be heard and in the same manner continues to react to stimuli whether visual, tactile, oral, olfactory, but is not subject to the same degree of rational conscious processing. The subject is not asleep or unconscious.

Information presented to the subconscious within this "state" will not be subject to the alterations of perception that are the mark of conscious processing of information and stimuli.

In stage hypnosis, this concept is often demonstrated by a suggestion such as that an onion given to the subject is in fact a juicy apple. The subconscious will accept the suggestion uninfluenced by the rational conscious mind. The subject will taste not an onion, but an apple.

Once trance "state" has been induced, then a process of deepening can be utilised, relaxing even more the constant chatter of the inner mind, allowing for therapeutic change to take place at a subconscious level.

Examples of deepening techniques are included in these pages. These techniques can be a very simple utilisation of a technique known as "compounding". Typical examples of this are: "as you experience X you can go ten times deeper into trance"; "I'm now going to take your right hand and, as I release it, it will fall into your lap just like a wet towel and you will go five times deeper into trance".

In order that we can facilitate changes in attitudes and behaviours, the therapeutic session continues using strategies that, when employed in conjunction with hypnosis, emulate recognised learning patterns. Suggestion therapy is very powerful, using positive affirmations that provide new and more beneficial responses to situations and conditions.

The practice of couching meaningful messages within metaphors was widely employed by the father of modern clinical hypnosis, Dr Milton Erickson. He used this technique as further distraction of conscious rationalisation while the important new learning was assimilated at a subconscious level. Hypnotherapy is in fact a teaching process, as we utilise the capabilities and the potential of the subconscious, taking advantage of our ever-increasing knowledge of learning patterns.

Whichever of the strategies is employed, they all have value and are effective. It is the skill and experience of the therapist in deciding which of the tactics available are most appropriate for his/her clients which will determine efficacy.

The hypnotherapy session concludes with a reorientation to conscious awareness, usually with a count. "I am now going to count from one to five and on the count of five you will be fully awake and aware". Of course, there is here an opportunity to give some suggestions such as: "On the count of five you will be fully awake and aware, feeling relaxed and comfortable as if you have had a refreshing nap". Discussion of the content of the therapy session is discouraged with the use of distractions such as, "What have you planned for the rest of the day?"

Within the scripts and strategies, I have included some italicised text. These items are for the guidance of the reader in his/her use in therapy, and I trust that these and the manner in which the material is presented will allow for easy understanding and utilisation.

A number of the scripts and strategies employ Neuro-Linguistic Programming (NLP) techniques. I would recommend that the reader take the opportunity to obtain some of the excellent works by Bandler & Grinder and by Andreas & Andreas on these concepts. I have included some of their works in the acknowledgements (at the end of this book), and they are available from most good book stores, or from the publishers of this book.

Inducing Hypnosis

It is my own belief that everyone can be hypnotized or, to be more accurate, that everyone is capable of attaining a state that we recognize as hypnosis. Much has been written by many learned theorists describing what is the hypnotic state, and I do not intend to allow myself to become embroiled in that particular debate. As a therapist I content myself with the fact that my clients are able to achieve a state that I am happy to describe as hypnosis, and that its use is of immense benefit as an adjunct to therapy. Entering this state is a natural ability that we all have, and we use it every day of our lives to enable us to focus attention.

When a first-time client is sitting in your consulting room, he/she will have brought to that session some preconceived ideas about hypnosis and those who use it in practice. In the main, their perceptions will probably have been shaped by the experience of watching a stage show. I find that it is always good practice to explore the perceptions of my clients to allay some of the fears that are usually present as a result of their experience.

"Will I be asleep?" I explain that they will be fully awake and fully conscious of everything that I say. "You will be very relaxed and comfortable and in effect the exact meaning of everything that I say to you will not concern you." I may then give an example as to how they have experienced hypnosis before, either by using the example of the television set and how everything else just fades into unimportance, or the example of the motorway journey when, having travelled at speed for some distance, there is a sudden realization that the conscious mind has not been fully involved in the driving. I'm sure that you will think of many similar examples that you can use.

"Will I do everything you tell me to do?" This should be recognized as the client's expression of their concern that they will not be in control, and that in some way you, the therapist, will have power over them. This is easily dealt with: I explain to my clients that they will be in complete control and that, if I were to suggest to them that they do something not within the realms of their normal moral code, either dangerous, illegal, or fattening, then quite simply they would not do it. Metaphors are always useful, and I often tell the story of how I went to see my bank manager in order to obtain funds for a particular project and how, having succumbed to my powers, he led me to the vaults telling me to just help myself. The point is usually effectively made!

Most of the questions are centred around this fear of losing control and so easily dealt with. It has to be sheer folly not to allow just a few minutes of the initial session to deal with this: it can save a lot of time later.

My usual preamble is contrived. I want that person sitting there in my therapy chair to accept my suggestions from the very outset. Just a small consideration will avoid the problem that so many call "resistance". "Okay Mary, what I would like you to do is make yourself very comfortable in that chair. Now would you prefer to go into hypnosis with your hands resting on a cushion in your lap or just resting on the arms of the chair?" (*Double bind*) "Now I realise that you will probably be wondering whether or not you will be able to go into hypnosis. If you just follow the simple instructions that I am going to give you, there is no way you can fail. Of course, you can resist me, but then that's not what you came for, is it?" In this way you will have established the rapport with your client that assures you of their compliance. Try it!

The first thing to do now is to achieve eye closure, and there are a few ways that you can do this. You can quite simply ask the client to close his/her eyes, but I myself prefer them to do it in their own time, with the thought that they are doing it because they want to go along with my suggestions.

I ask the client to look at a spot on my hand as I hold it just above their normal line of sight so that they have to strain their eyes upwards.

Eye Closure

"Now Mary, I want you to just pick a spot on the palm of my hand and just focus your eyes on that spot. You may notice that it is rather uncomfortable focusing your eyes on that spot and that it would be so nice to just close them, but I really don't want you not to close your eyes too quickly. You may notice how quickly your eyes begin to tire and become heavy, but that is fine; just focus on that spot as you listen to the sound of my voice. Nothing bothers you or disturbs you now as you listen to the sound of my voice, and the words that I say relax you .... and as I bring my hand down past your eyes you can follow that hand down past your nose...down past your mouth .... down under your chin, allowing them to close quite naturally .... closing now .... closing .... closing .... and that's fine .... I wouldn't want you to know now how much more comfortable you can feel as your eyes relax and you relax, completely in control now as you allow my words to just wash over you, each word relaxing you more and more."

(To continue, go to appropriate induction)

From this point on, it does not matter if you are reading from a script. After all, your client's eyes are closed and he/she cannot see what you are doing. Very soon now, as the trance state continues, they will not be concerned one jot, just comfortably relaxed. However, do not ignore your client: make sure you keep one eye on them to ensure that all is going well with them.

Voice modulation is important, and it can be very difficult to explain just how to deliver a hypnotic induction. I have used "...." to indicate pauses in the text, and would suggest that if you speak in a manner which is flowing and soft, reducing the speed of your delivery to about 70% of your normal speech rate, then you will not go too far amiss. Experience and practice will of course make perfect.

The technique above is the one that I use most frequently with my clients. However, there are many other techniques designed to achieve rapid eye closure which are equally effective. Some of these techniques have specific application such as working with children or anxious clients. There follows a number of these, as well as a technique for obtaining self-hypnosis.

Roger P. Allen

Two Finger Eye Closure

An induction for adults:

Now (*client's name*), ... Take a long deep breath .... now just open your eyes wide, looking upwards towards your eyebrows, without straining your neck .... Now I am going to pull down your eyelids ... shut .... like this (use thumb and forefinger to gently close the eyelids). Now I want you to relax those muscles right there under my fingers .... just allow them to relax .... Relax them to the point where they just do not want to work .... and when you are sure that you have done that for yourself .... relaxed those muscles completely to the point where they just will not work .... then satisfy yourself .... have a try and find your eyes locking tighter and tighter .... (wait about 3 to 4 seconds.) .... That's fine .... there is no need to test them any further. Now you can allow that feeling .... that relaxation, to flow down through your body .... relaxing every muscle ... every fibre ... all the way down to the tips of your toes.

I am going to lift up your right hand now ... and shake, gently shake, relaxation into that hand ... that arm ... and when I release that arm, it will fall back into your lap just like a wet towel ... and you will go ten times deeper into relaxation. (Repeat with left arm.)

I have found this technique to be very effective when dealing with a sceptical client. It provides the client with proof that they have entered a trance state by not being able to open their eyes. The arm-drop test also provides an excellent deepening technique.

Children Up To The Age Of 10

(Begin in a conversational manner; it may help if you can find out what is the child's favourite toy.)

Now John, ... I expect that you play a lot with your toys at home .... I bet that you have a lot of toys and that when you play with them you pretend that they are real .... don't you ? .... I know that I did, when I was a little boy like you. Well .... you know we have a game of pretend here too .... and if you learn this game with me ... nothing that will happen here today will bother you at all. Would you like to learn this game? I'm sure you would.

Okay now John, ... let's start by taking a big deep breath in .... and then let it all out .... Now you can open your eyes just as wide as you can and I am going to show you this game of pretend. Now I am going to pull your eyelids closed .... like this .... (*Finger & thumb technique*) and you can pretend that you just can't open your eyes .... that's all you have to do .... just pretend as hard as you can that you just can't open your eyes no matter what .... pretend so hard that when you try to open your eyes ... they just won't work at all .... now try to make them work when you are pretending like that .... the more you try, the more they will not work because you are pretending so hard .... and because you are so good at pretending. Nothing that happens now will bother you or disturb you at all .... in your mind, you can be at home playing with your favourite toys ... and you need not concern yourself with anything else at all ....

Concept : David Elman

Fractional Induction

A general purpose induction:

As you rest so quietly there, just listening to the sound of my voice, I would like you now to concentrate on your feet and your toes. Concentrate on the muscles of your feet and feel any tension there in those muscles .... hold that tension .... and now just let it go .... allowing those muscles to soften and to loosen as you relax those muscles completely, letting go of tension .... letting go of anxiety now.

Now concentrate on the muscles of your ankles .... your calves and your knees, becoming aware now of the tension in those muscles .... feel that tension there .... hold that tension .... and now just let it all go .... allowing those muscles to soften and to loosen .... relaxing .... releasing .... just letting go as you listen to the sounds of my voice .... nothing bothers you or concerns you .... each word that I utter is just a signal for you to relax and go deeper .... and, as you go deeper now, you can become aware of the large muscles of your thighs .... feel the tension in those muscles .... feel the tightness here and then just let it go .... those large muscles softening .... loosening .... lengthening, as all the tension just drains away now .... as relaxation continues .... If you have done this correctly, you will become aware of that comfortable heaviness as your legs relax.

Now allow that heaviness and relaxation to move into the muscles of your ~~buttocks and your pelvic~~ region, all tension draining down now like the fine black sand in an hour-glass .... down into the bottom of the glass .... the passing of time .... time to relax and allow those comfortable feelings to continue as those muscles release all tension .... soften .... lengthen and loosen, and you drift deeper and deeper as my voice drifts with you now.

Now become aware of the muscles of your stomach and of your lower back .... feel the tension in those muscles .... and as you release that tension and those muscles relax ... soften .... lengthen .... loosen, you go deeper still as your body relaxes and your mind relaxes with it into peace and tranquillity, but now I really wouldn't want you to relax too quickly .... it's so much easier for you to allow that feeling to continue as you listen to the sounds of my voice .... the sounds in the room, and you can recognize that ability that is yours, to relax, and to reflect on your problems in a certain way.

Aware now of those muscles in your chest and your back .... aware of your breathing .... aware now of how relaxed and how quiet your breathing has become .... with each gentle breath you breathe out tension .... breathe out anxiety .... then breathe in peace .... harmony .... a feeling of security as muscles release their tension .... softening and loosening as you drift ever deeper .... feeling so comfortable and so good.

Now become aware of the muscles of your arms your hands, your shoulders, as you allow that relaxation to continue, relaxing each muscle, releasing tension, that comfortable heaviness continuing now, and it really can seem now to be too much effort to try even to make the effort to move those arms that are so heavy now as you listen to that voice speaking to you in soothing tones that relax you even deeper. Now the muscles of your neck .... feel the tension here .... now let it go and feel your neck shorten, as those muscles soften .... lengthen .... loosen .... all tension draining away now as your conscious mind becomes more and more comfortable and your unconscious mind assumes more and more of the responsi- bility for guiding and directing your thoughts .... your responses, as you allow this trance to continue.

Now become aware of the muscles of your face .... your jaw .... allow those muscles to just sag now as you release all of that tension .... your teeth slightly apart .... you feel the tip of your tongue now just brushing the back of your teeth as you drift still deeper .... relaxing .... releasing .... just letting go completely.

That feeling of relaxation can continue now into the muscles of your scalp .... the furrows of your forehead smooth over now as all tension just drains away and your entire body relaxes .... drifting in space .... that free floating place of effortless letting go as you now begin to use this opportunity to learn even more about your ability to relax .... and to let go completely .... as you drift into this trance more and more deeply .... more and more effortlessly .... and I continue to talk to you.

You can judge at this point whether you need to use a deepener script or continue with the session as you have planned.

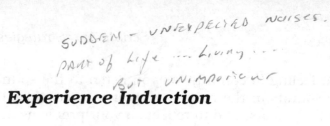

SUDDEN - UNEXPECTED NOISES.
PART of Life ... Living ...
BuT UNIMPORTANT

Experience Induction

This induction is appropriate for anxious clients. Contra-indication: clients who have a fear of water.

Now you are resting comfortably THERE, listening to the sound of my voice HERE, with your eyes closed comfortably, you can be aware of your eyes and of how you are in control .... and how you could open them should you wish .... and that's fine, because I really wouldn't want you to not go into hypnosis *TRANCE* too quickly, I would prefer that you discover how much easier it is simply to allow events to occur in their own time and in their own way .... and as you allow that feeling to continue in a shoulder .... a leg .... a hand, as you continue to listen to the sound of my voice .... the sounds that surround you .... the ticking of the clock perhaps or the distant murmur of traffic .... paying close attention now to those feelings .... those changes as they occur, as you wonder at your own ability to let go completely and drift into a trance, while your conscious mind has already begun to drift off somewhere else .... allowing the body to relax and the mind to relax .... without knowing at all how much more comfortable and relaxed you can become.

I wonder if you can remember now those experiences of drifting off whilst sitting comfortably watching television .... so engrossed in the story line .... listening to the voices as your eyes closed to rest quietly for a moment in time .... hearing the music .... or those words spoken .... in that quiet and relaxed way ... when a word or a sound brings to mind a particular memory .... and you drift into that memory .... dream away for a time .... come back to the words again .... until the words and the music become a soothing murmur .... a relaxing sound .... heard only in the background of the mind .... like a conversation overheard .... a peaceful and quiet time .... and the subconscious part of your mind continues to hear all that is important to you .... whilst your conscious mind drifts off to another place without really noticing that there is no need for you to make the effort to try .... to hear .... or to understand every-thing that is said or not said HERE .... as you rest so quietly .... THERE. You really have known all along how much easier it is to learn when you are so relaxed .... though I wouldn't want you to relax too quickly at first .... I would prefer that you discover now how much easier it is to recognize the small changes .... tiny changes .... almost imperceptible changes .... happening in your breathing .... and in your pulse .... how quiet and comfortable you have become as that feeling of security relaxes you even deeper than before. Your unconscious may choose to relax just one of your fingers before it continues to relax one of your thumbs .... or perhaps it will discover that your wrist will be a handier place to begin relaxing, but the conscious of your mind can enjoy being curious about exactly where those feelings will begin.

And now (*client's name*), please consider a stone being skipped across the clear calm surface of a pond .... the stone skips once .... twice .... three times and more .... each time the intervals shorter as it loses momentum .... slowing .... down more and more .... As it strikes the surface the peace and tranquillity is disturbed .... the water flows in ripples that spread in perfect rings .... but then the stone can skip no more .... all momentum is dissipated, its power lost .... and so it slips quietly down beneath the surface .... gently floating down .... past the creatures that live here .... drifting down .... gently ... quietly .... past the water plants .... and nothing is disturbed as it finally comes to rest there .... still now on the bottom of the tranquil pool .... and on the surface .... even the ripples become quieter as they spread in ever increasing circles .... to disappear entirely as the surface becomes calm again, and you can take the opportunity to quietly reflect upon those problems as you recognize now that ability that is yours .... to relax .... to let go of tension .... anxiety .... aware now of your ability to see things in a different way .... and to accept those things that seemed to be one thing and then turn out to be something else entirely .... and then the difficulty and ease that can be your experience, telling the difference between souls and soles .... sun and son .... bear and bare .... changing old beliefs .... recognizing new capabilities and capacities .... learning new ways of doing things.

I wonder now if you can allow those feelings to continue .... the same .... or to deepen even more now as you try to remember all those things I have said here .... about that pool there .... that television .... that stone that drifted down slowly .... even as you drift with your own thoughts .... and enjoy allowing that pleasant and comfortable experience of heaviness of arms .... of legs .... to continue there now as I continue to talk to you .... each word that I speak .... relaxing you deeper still.

You can judge at this point whether you need to use a deepener script or continue with the session as you have planned.

Question Of Reality

An induction to dissociate and observe reality:

I wonder if you have considered .... how to judge what's real ....

How do you make sense of it all?

Is it by what you see? .... That part that you consciously see?

Is it by what you hear with your ears? .... That part that you consciously hear?

And what you can feel with your touch? .... That part which you consciously know you are touching?

Or do you realise reality by the sense your subconscious makes?

Those feelings you feel on the inside?

Those sounds from within .... to you .... from you?

Those pictures in your mind?

Does your right hand know what your left hand is doing?

How do you create what is real?

And .... how else could you do that?

How many other flavours to reality do you think there might be .... which you can add to what you already taste? .... And .... which works best for you, and when?

You know, by how comfortable you feel.

Like a prism turning a single ray of light .... to a rainbow of colour .... your imagination is a prism for experience .... both past and future .... through which to perceive your present .... ponder your past .... anticipate your future.

And since it is your imagination, your senses can to create what is so.

So what would you like to create? Or should it be "who"?

Knowing that you determine what you experience .... and .... the meaning of the outcome .... you can choose to perceive those things which you enjoy .... which make you feel comfortable .... and/or .... learn more effectively .... from experience, either past or present, or future.

Self-Hypnosis Training Script

"There is an old saying, "If you give a man a fish, you have given him a meal. If you teach him how to fish you have given him a liveli-hood.

"Teaching those whom you work with is a means for insuring that your clients can continue to work independently and grow in your absence."

Michael Yapko, 1990

And now as I speak to you .... I wonder if you can close your eyes and remember those experiences of hypnosis that you have had before .... how easy it became to relax with those words spoken to you .... soft, soothing words that allowed you to let go of tension .... let go of cares as you drifted with those words and with your own thoughts too .... but today I would like you to know that you have that capability to go into trance and to utilize that experience completely by yourself .... not needing to know more about how to allow this alteration to occur .... and you can do this at any time that you want to or need to .... to allow you to use the abilities that are there for you as they have always been .... there in your perfect unconscious mind that can do so many things for you.

All you need to do is concentrate now on all of the muscles of your face .... and screw up those muscles so tight .... closing your eyes so tight .... and then feel that tension there .... feel that tension in your jaw .... in the muscles of your neck .... in your shoulders .... that tension spreading right down through your arms to the very tips of your fingers .... I would like you to really feel that tension and be intensely aware of the tightness and the discomfort in those muscles .... now hold it .... hold that tension .... and now I want you to count to three, and on the count of three .... release that tension, let it go completely .... your eyes remaining shut comfortably as all of the tension in all of those muscles just flows away now .... begin to count now with me .... 1 .... 2 .... 3 (*match breathing count on outward breath*) .... R-E-L-A-X .... that's good .... very good .... relaxing releasing .... letting go completely as every muscle relaxes and you drift down with that relaxation as it occurs .... allowing that comfort-able heaviness to increase .... to flow down .... softening .... each muscle loosening as that relaxation increases now .... You can continue to drift down as you allow that trance to deepen now as you remember all that you experienced before .... that feeling of comfort .... of security perhaps .... as you relax each and every small part of you .... allowing the subconscious of your mind to accept the responsibility for taking care of those things that are important to you .... as your conscious mind drifts to wherever it wishes to .... perhaps to a special place that your subconscious will provide for you .... where you can relax even deeper .... secure .... safe .... enjoying that pleasant feeling of experiences of trance remembered .... where you can utilize those experiences that can help you .... and as you drift down .... then so you can drift back again .... in your own time as you choose when your attention is required or just when you want to .... drifting back to full wakeful awareness as your eyes open .... and you can take this opportunity to practise again your ability to create your own state of comfortable hypnosis .... creating that tension, as before .... feeling that tension, that discomfort .... and then .... counting to three .... to release that tension .... and allow that trance to develop and to continue .... as you allow that drifting down .... deeper and deeper .... each breath of yours relaxing you more .... that experience of yours continuing as you allow it to .... and I would like you to continue now to practise that ability .... to drift down .... to enjoy that experience and then to drift back again .... so go ahead now while I sit here quietly and wait for you .... that's very good.

(Allow a minute or two to elapse and then continue)

I am very impressed, (*client's name*); you have learned very well how to do that for yourself .... how to create that tension .... and then to release that tension .... and to drift down into a comfortable state of self-hypnosis where you can utilize the abilities and capacities that your subconscious mind can provide for you .... that creative part of you, where those special capabilities and capacities will be available to you even more than before .... your subconscious mind can do so many things for you .... as you drift down into that trance in your own time and in your own way .... to ask that your unconscious provide those things needed for you .... aware that all that you need to do is to relax in that way .... and ask it to do so .... and then to drift back up again .... in your own time .... in your own way .... bringing with you those comfortable positive feelings of balance .... of things resolved .... feeling refreshed .... as you reach the surface of wakeful awareness .... allowing your eyes to open .... as you take a deep breath and smile.

Have your subject practise this procedure once or twice before leaving the office, and emphasis the need to practise this new skill for their own benefit during the whole of their life.

Deepeners:

The Candle

Now as you relax more, and let go more and more, you can allow every muscle in your body to relax.

Now picture in your mind, a candle .... this candle can be any colour you wish it to be. The colour that you have chosen for your candle is a colour that your subconscious knows relaxes you and calms your mind.

Now focus on the flame of the candle. See how beautiful the colours within the flame are. You may see red, blue, yellow, purple, white or maybe another colour, and as you see the colours within the flame, you relax more and go deeper, as you enjoy these heavy and relaxed feelings, these hypnotic feelings.

Now focus on the wax body of your candle. As you see the first trickle of melting wax, begin to move down the side of this warm and comfortable candle.

Now see the melting wax touch the candle holder and merge with it to become part of the candle holder .... You become more and more relaxed, safe and comfortable.

Now imagine that you are that candle, a candle of total relaxation and, as you picture it, as a particular muscle in your body, helping you to relax more and more completely. Picture the chair that you are sitting in, as a candle holder, and that your muscles, like the wax of your candle of relaxation, are melting into the chair and that you are becoming, yourself, a candle of relaxation.

Anon

A gentle deepener, ideal where a light trance is required.

The Mind's Eye

"In the same way that you have eyes that see the world around you, you also have an inner eye that we call "the mind's eye".... and it can see images and process thoughts even as you relax so deeply .... and the mind's eye has an eyelid and, like your physical eye, that eyelid can close down .... as it too becomes heavy and tired ... wanting to close .... and it can begin to close .... and, as it slowly drops, it shuts out stray thoughts .... stray images, and can leave your mind perfectly clear .... it experiences whatever you would choose .... and it's closing now .... closing more and more ... and you mind grows quiet and at peace .... and now it closes completely ... .. closing out all stray thoughts or images that you don't want to interfere with how relaxed you are ...."

Michael Yapko, 1990

An extremely effective technique, that can be utilized to "damp down" the continual internal self speak, allowing for deeper trance experience.

The Garden

As you go deeper now .... your subconscious mind becomes open .... more accessible and receptive to new learnings .... to changing old beliefs .... as you relax so comfortably there .... just listening to the sound of my voice .... here .... so calm .... a feeling of peace and tranquillity .... allows you to relax more and more .... with each easy breath .... with each gentle beat of your heart.

As I count down from ten to one .... you can just let go and you can go deeper now .... with each count .... using each number to let go of stress and tension .... to go deeper now.

Ten .... As you allow each muscle and nerve in your body to relax .... letting go .... becoming calm .... you feel peaceful .... comfortable now.

Nine .... You relax your mind and your body together .... and if you lose track of the progression of the numbers .... then that's fine .... just let go now .... as ....

Eight .... You start to sense a gentle connection between your mind and your body .... and an inner wisdom.

Seven .... Go deeper now .... and as you breathe out .... *(Start to pace with breathing)* .... start to breathe out fear .... breathing out anxiety now.

Six .... Letting fear .... anger and stress flow away from your body .... with every outward breath .... letting go now .... slowly .... comfortably .... calmly.

Five .... And now with each outward breath .... I want you to start saying a word to yourself .... without moving your mouth or your tongue .... your breathing not changing .... your throat perfectly still .... on each outward breath .... say the word inwardly to yourself .... CALM .... *(pace with outward breath, and repeat.)* .... CALM.

Four .... Without thinking what it means .... without analysing the word .... just moving the sound inward now .... so that it seems to come from an inner wisdom .... *(continue to match breathing)* .... CALM.

Three .... Gently now .... easily .... calmly .... calm .... letting go .... and whenever your mind strays from that sound .... and it will stray away .... then just acknowledge that fact and gently bring it back .... repeating to yourself the word .... CALM .... *(matching breathing)*.

Two .... Continuing now to relax .... and to let go .... gently drifting down .... into peace and harmony of body .... mind .... and spirit.

One .... And as you continue to drift deeper still .... you begin to see .... sense or imagine yourself in a beautiful garden .... the sun is shining .... gently warming your skin .... comfortable .... you look across the lawn as it sweeps away to an ornamental pond .... with a fountain playing .... the water droplets sparkling .... glistening .... in the soft, diffused light that filters down through the leaves and branches of the ancient trees that surround this garden .... shielding and sheltering this beautiful place.

TROUBLE   TREE

The grass is soft .... springy beneath your feet, and as you walk .... you pass flower beds cut into the lawn .... filled with the most beautiful flowers and plants .... so many varieties and colours .... and you can be aware of the fragrance of the flowers carried to you on a soft breeze that drifts across the garden .... rustling the leaves .... causing the heads of the flowers to sway gently .... the subtle sound of nature all around .... birds singing .... the drone of insects and the splash and gurgle of cascading water .... each sound .... each sensation relaxing you more .... comforting as you drift deeper .... and every step becoming heavier.

You soon find yourself in a small clearing .... the sun warming you and relaxing you more and more now .... as you sit .... resting your back against a large and ancient tree .... the bark of the tree is soft and comfortable .... and you sense that many people have rested here as you are resting now .... but although you are alone .... you feel safe here .... peaceful .... comfortable .... the word CALM .... comforts you more as your mind drifts and fades. Script now

This is perhaps one of the most frequently used deepeners in use. However before using this technique do check with your client first that they have no aversions to gardens or have problems with hay fever or similar allergies. If they do then use another more appropriate technique.

Continue with session as planned.

The Stair

Now you can allow your inner mind to show you standing at the top of a fine marble staircase, with ten steps leading down. There is a firm handrail and here you feel safe and secure .... nothing concerns you at all. In a moment you can walk down that staircase and as you hear me count off each of the steps, you can step down one step .... doubling your relaxation with each step you take.

Begin now as I count .... Ten .... Doubling your relaxation going deeper *(pace with breathing)* .... Nine .... Deeper still .... Eight .... Letting go of tension as you relax and go deeper. .... Seven .... Doubling your relaxation .... deeper still .... Six .... Aware now of your breathing and how comfortable it has become .... Five .... Each gentle breath relaxes you .... you relax more with each breath that you take .... Four .... Deeper .... even deeper into a state of profound relaxation of mind and body .... Three .... Doubling your relaxation going ever deeper .... Two .... The deeper you go, the better you feel .... and the better you feel, the deeper you go .... One .... Almost all the way down now into total relaxation .... Zero .... Now stepping off the bottom step and you can find yourself in a place that is comfortable and safe for you to be .... a place of safety and security where there is no anxiety .... no fear .... just tranquillity .... and calm peace.

This is a really effective technique favoured by many therapists. It is popular as it matches the internal state of the client and their rate of breathing to your words. Very occasionally you may find a client breathing increasingly more deeply with each count that you make. If this occurs just say "breathe comfortably, only as deeply as you need to relax even more deeply ...." and then return to counting.

Continue with session as planned

Suggestion Therapy:

Ideomotor Response
(I.M.R.)

There are many occasions in therapy where it is necessary to ask the client questions and to receive answers. It is a widely held belief that asking the client to speak can interfere with the depth of the trance. So, in order to avoid this, the client is asked to communicate via finger movements to signal yes or no. This technique is known as ideomotor response.

As you relax comfortably .... you can be aware of the fact that going deeply into hypnosis is a rewarding and pleasant experience, and that any discomfort that you may feel will only occur in the context of the therapy .... and only if I direct you to.

Now I want you allow yourself to go even deeper .... drifting down into a state of profound relaxation of mind and body .... sensing now a gentle connection between your mind .... your body and your innermost self. With each breath that you take you relax deeper into peace and calm .... tranquillity.

And now I want to speak to that part of you which is all-knowing .... knows all about (*client's name*) .... and forgets nothing .... and which never tells a lie.

I will from time to time be asking questions that require a yes or no answer .... you can answer me by allowing the pointing finger of your right hand to lift if the answer to my question is Yes. I will now touch that finger (Touch finger) .... If the answer to my question is No, then you can allow me to know by allowing the pointing finger of your left hand to lift. I will now touch that finger. (*Touch Finger.*) (*Repeat Paragraph*).

Should you not know the answer to my question, or wish not to divulge this to me, then you can indicate this to me by allowing both of the pointing fingers of your right and your left hand to lift simultaneously.

Roger P. Allen

(Client's name) need know nothing of this as he/she communicates with me verbally, reporting to me those thoughts and feelings …. images …. events as are necessary for the purposes of this therapy.

Do you understand the instructions that I have given to you? *(Watch for response).*

Continue with session as planned.

Sports Performance

As you prepare to (*engage in or play sport*), allow your imagination to show you a scene, a familiar place perhaps, or one that you can create for yourself, it does not matter at all, as long as you can find this place restful and strengthening, a place where you would choose to be if you felt a bit low or depressed and you wanted to feel better.

If you wish, you can choose to have somebody there with you, someone special to you who makes you feel good, who gives you strength and purpose. This person may be a brother or a sister, mother or father or someone who is very close to you. It may be someone whom you admire from afar, living or otherwise. By doing this and allowing yourself to experience that place and that person, you are choosing a place and a person who strengthens and motivates you to your maximum potential.

Some can draw strength from a scene such as a candle flickering, a watermill turning, or a bonfire, or a mountain stream as it rushes over the rocks. It matters not, as long as it is a scene which provides for you an inner peace and tranquillity and gives to you a special feeling of confidence and inner strength of purpose.

So now (*client's name*) .... imagine yourself at that place and, at peace with your own inner self, or with that special person, and allow that special feeling of calm and confidence, of tranquillity of spirit to grow and to expand, as you experience it, breathe in the essence of it, breathe in the clear air, absorb the powerful and positive vibrations, and, with each breath, you can feel that strength and purpose, feel your mental and physical being strengthening.

Experience now that surge of energy pulsing through your body as your powers centralize, as your mind focuses intently on the task at hand, your concentration and your energies vibrating and pulsing with positive intent and purpose, your mind and body in perfect tune as you prepare for that moment when all of your energies physical and mental will integrate with the finely honed skills and techniques and burst forth in perfect harmony and unison, as your mind sees you completing the (*race,task, performance*) ...... achieving your goal, a winner, a champion. As you do this feel yourself gaining in strength and health, increasing your vitality, taking all that you need physically and mentally from this experience, feeling better and stronger, more alive, more confident in your ability to achieve, to win, to overcome.

Practise this for just a few minutes each and every day, actually drawing the strength and the vitality, both physically and mentally from whatever helps you. Know that you can do all that you need to do, whatever you want to do, whatever you believe you can do. You can do it, if you allow your mind to accept that you can do it. You can do anything that you want to do if you want it enough and you believe in your own abilities and capacities for greatness and for achievement.

Practise this and then practise some more, for a few minutes each and every day, practise to train your mind to give you the best opportunity and the positive belief in your ability to prevail. Once you have done that, you can relax, confident and assured in the knowledge that you have prepared yourself in the most effective and diligent way possible to be the best that you can be, the best that you can ask yourself to be. Know and believe that, if it is attainable, if it is realistic, then it is achievable, what your mind can conceive, it can achieve. Whatever you believe, you can achieve. Work on believing it and as you believe it it will be so and you will achieve.

When you are in competition, before you make a single move, you can visualize in your mind a successful outcome. Visualize what you wish to happen happening for you, what you need to do to do well, for you to succeed.

Practise doing this every day as part of your training and preparation, and never make a move when you are actually competing without visualizing a successful outcome. Concentrate on what will happen next, in the next few minutes or the next few seconds. What happened before does not concern you at all, it is of no value to you as you shut out from your mind all that is not important to you in your quest for excellence. Visualize with all your strength and concentrate on only that which is important, the present moment and the immediate future, on what will happen next. You will shut out all that is unimportant and irrelevant, concentrating on that special moment, as all of your abilities and strengths concentrate and unite in perfect harmony, providing for you the perfect balance of concentration, of positive tension and calmness and clarity of thought, your body and mind perfectly attuned to provide you with maximum and most effective concentration of effort both physically and mentally.

You will concentrate on that future and concentrate on making it happen. You have all that you need to perform at your very best and you know that you will perform to your highest potential. You have excellent powers of judgment, your decision-making will be at its optimum performance, you will be clear and definite, and in excellent form both mentally and physically, you will have all of the determination, confidence and the stamina to perform at your best and for as long as you need to in order to achieve your highest potential. You believe in yourself, believe in your ability, whatever you do you will do well and you will do it better than you have ever done it before. You now believe yourself to be a winner. You are a winner.

Pass Your Driving Test

As you go deeper now .... each breath relaxing you more .... you can imagine it is time for you to demonstrate your ability and skills as a driver .... knowing that you are going to be successful. What usually occurs is that which you expect .... and you expect that you will be calm .... confident .... relaxed and in complete control. You expect that you will pass your test easily and without effort .... and you know now that what you thought could be difficult .... will be so very easy because you are relaxed and in the perfect frame of mind to succeed.

When you are called upon to demonstrate your skill as a driver you will be calm .... confident .... and completely relaxed.

You will be so pleasantly surprised at the ease with which you will maintain your calm and confident manner .... as you demonstrate your skills and your abilities as a driver .... you will be amazed that something you had thought would be difficult .... will be so very very easy .... it will be easy because you will be completely relaxed and calm .... and in this relaxed and calm .... confident state you will be in the perfect frame of mind .... you will be successful .... you will pass your driving test.

Now *(client's name)*, I want you to visualize as vividly as you can these following scenes that I will suggest to you. Every day .... I want you to practise visualizing these scenes .... imagine them as vividly as you can .... and in every scene you are calm .... confident .... and relaxed.

You are now in the car driving to the test centre. After completing the necessary formalities .... you emerge from the test centre with your examiner .... and you walk towards your car. You now sit in the car and make all of the necessary checks and adjustments before you start the engine.

Now you are driving the car and doing all of those things that you have learned .... you perform each and every stage of your driving extremely well. Imagine yourself .... carrying out a three point turn .... excellent .... Now reversing around a corner .... keeping just the right distance from the kerb .... perfectly ....

Now imagine yourself parking the car between two other vehicles .... taking your time .... judging the distance just right .... parking beautifully .... excellent.

Now imagine yourself performing an emergency stop .... braking the vehicle to a halt quickly and with complete safety .... perfectly.

Now imagine yourself doing a hill start .... balancing engine .... clutch and hand brake absolutely perfectly .... pulling way smoothly .... very good! Imagine yourself driving in traffic .... keeping a proper distance .... using your mirrors .... observing and giving proper consideration to all other road users .... driving safely and smoothly .... with anticipation and confidence .... knowing that you are competent and have studied and practised until you are perfect.

Practise visualizing these scenes as vividly as you can throughout the day as often as you can .... in the morning .... when settling down for the night .... whenever you have some time to yourself .... seeing yourself at all times .... calm .... confident .... and relaxed.

You have studied the Highway Code .... all of the information that you need is there in your memory because you have made the effort to study .... all of this information will spring instantly to mind and to your lips at the moment when you need it .... so see yourself right now .... answering questions on the Highway Code .... see yourself answering each question easily and fluently .... answering every question correctly .... and you expect to be right .... perfect!

Now imagine the examiner .... telling you that you have passed the test .... congratulating you .... handing you a piece of paper confirming that you are now a qualified driver.

When you actually take your test .... you will have taken your test so many times in your mind, it will be like something that you have done before many times .... with great skill and confidence .... in reality it will happen just as you have practised in your mind.

You will find it easy to produce a polished and accomplished demonstration of your driving skills .... You are going to pass your test .... you are going to pass your driving test with consummate ease.

You will be aware of a voice that speaks to you from within .... as you take your driving test .... you will hear the calm and comforting voice of the skillful driver within you .... that voice will calm you .... it will relax you.

Please practise your visualizations as many times as you can throughout your day .... visualize each and every step .... each action .... each procedure .... do it in the morning .... do it before you retire at night .... in every scene see yourself .... calm .... confident .... and relaxed .... skillful .... and knowledgeable.

You have done all that you need to pass your driving test .... you have prepared yourself physically .... you have practised all the skills and the techniques that are necessary .... you have the experience .... you have done it all many times successfully .... you have studied the Highway Code .... you are prepared mentally and physically .... just believe that you can pass and you will pass your driving test ....

Now go .... and pass your driving test.

Metaphors:

Emelda

This metaphor was written especially for Kay, a young lady of 28 years who was causing her now retired parents much distress through her ever increasing demands on them. The purpose of the therapy was to allow her to realise at a subconscious level that she was responsible for her own life and that her demands were unreasonable.

I am reminded of a story about a very wealthy landowner who many years ago was famous for his kindness and generosity to those who were in his service. He had many servants and retainers, and, for their benefit, he established a fine home where they could live in comfort and security in their old age.

He had two daughters of whom he was very proud as a father should be and doted on them both, giving to them all of his love, for he had lost his own wife, their mother, in childbirth when the younger daughter was born. The elder of the daughters was of a loving and kind disposition, taking after her father, and was soon married to a prince who took her far away.

The other daughter was a concern to her father who noted well her manner of always getting her own way through her disruptive behaviour and manipulative ways. But he loved her and in his concern for her he charged one of his most trusted servants and the servant's wife that they should take care of her and be responsible for her well-being on his death.

Although the daughter was not best loved by the servants, the man concerned gave his pledge to his master that he would indeed ensure that the rich man's daughter was looked after.

The rich man provided for the couple a generous income and a comfortable home across the valley so that they could live in comfort in return for their watching over the daughter and ensuring that no harm came to her.

Eventually the rich man died, and, as he had no son, his daughter inherited from him half of his wealth and the great manor house and all it contained. Now the work of the servant and his wife began. In her fashion, the daughter devised a complex manner of ensuring that the retainer and his wife would always be at her beck and call, for were they not responsible for her, had they not promised her father?

On the top of the mansion house walls, she caused to be installed a great drum and a huge horn, the beat and the note of which were such that they would fill the valley with her calls, and none would escape the noise of her demands. Also was erected here a large flag-pole from which she could fly banners which demanded the attention of the retainer and his wife.

Her calls were loud and many and her manner towards the faithful retainer and his wife became ever more abusive. But the promise to take on the responsibility for the daughter's well-being had been given by an honourable man. Without complaint he took from her the responsibility of her own well-being. Many were the times when he and his wife would trek across the valley to answer her calls, to draw the water from the well and to cut the wood for the fire, to cook and to clean as she wasted her life, lay in her bed, growing larger and less attractive to those who would woo her for her wealth, indulging herself at the expense of those who now loved her not as they had loved her father.

As the retainer and his wife grew older, so they became more frail and the work of their demanding mistress became too much. They asked for help, that their mistress might employ others to help them, but her reply was, "Whose responsibility is it to look after me?" They received no consideration at all. As the old man grew more frail and more slow, then the beating of the drum and the blast of the horn grew louder and more insistent, and all in the valley heard the clamour of her demands and kept away.

But the old retainer and his wife, ever faithful to their promise, struggled ever on to do their best. Slowly and painfully they kept to the task, now to be beaten for their slowness and abused with the lash of the woman's tongue for their failing strength. Those who ran the home for the elderly ex-servants of the rich man tried in vain to persuade them both to give up their charge, for they had done their duty, done their best and without gratitude or consideration.

"Come now and enjoy the retirement that you have earned, take on that responsibility which can only be yours, while you can still stand on your own two feet, and allow others to take on the responsibility which never was yours and can never be removed from that person who is responsible for that life." But the old man persevered, for he had given a pledge.

The day came when the drums were beating and the horn blasts filled the air with their demanding row, but the onset of age had dimmed the eyes and the hearing of the old couple, and for them the world was quiet and peaceful, time to enjoy the loving company that had been the mainstay of their marriage.

The daughter fumed and raged; the noise was horrendous, but to no avail. She called for her carriage and at a breakneck pace rode to the cottage where the old couple had lived at her beck and call for these many years. Her years of self-indulgence were apparent now, her gluttony immersing her former beauty within a now grotesque body, her face livid with rage and hatred at this unforgivable lapse in the attention to her whim. She crashed through the door. Within the old man dozed in the chair by the fire as his wife, now hobbling with the aid of a stick, busied herself with the preparation of their evening meal. Her rage was enormous as she lashed out with her cane, striking the old man from his chair, cursing the elderly couple with the language of the gutter as she set about them in her tantrum. Even though she recognized the frailty of those who had taken so much responsibility for her, she would show no consideration, and so she smashed and destroyed the things that were precious within that home, screaming her rage at the world. It was the coachman who saved them more hurt. He seized the struggling Emelda and threw her back into the coach. He then drove her back to the big house, and locked her in her room to allow her temper and rage to subside. He took care of the horses as he had done for so many years and then packed up his few possessions and left, never to return.

The home over the mountain had two new residents the following day, for those who were concerned came and they fetched the old couple away from harm. Now they would live the remainder of their lives in the peace and harmony they deserved, that responsibility so long misplaced now firmly laid where it belonged. They would enjoy the sunshine and the softening glow of eventide in the evening of their lives, looking not back at those years so cruelly taken from them, now responsible only for themselves, having done their best and more.

And what of the daughter? What happened to her? Who would care now? WHO WOULD TAKE RESPONSIBILITY FOR HER LIFE AND WELL-BEING NOW?

Perhaps she did make the effort to put aside old ways and to listen to that wise inner voice; perhaps she accepted the responsibility for her own life; perhaps she looked from within herself to others and thereby grew as a special and unique person, to become part of life as it is and to enjoy what there is.

I hope that she will be OKAY; I wonder what you think? WILL SHE BE OKAY?

Bicycles

This metaphor was written specifically for a young lady who had been with her fiancé for a number of years and was now finding herself attracted to another man at work. He was the complete opposite of her fiance, extroverted and brash, devil-may-care. He had shown an interest in our heroine, but then he had shown an interest in so many others before. How was she to choose what was true reality?

As you relax more and more .... the mind can wander at times the way that nomads wander from place to place .... never going anywhere special, just drifting from here to there .... which can sound so romantic and so relaxing too .... unless there is something you want to do or somewhere that you want to go .... something that really is important for you to have .... because it really can be difficult to arrive at your goal if you do not know where you are going .... don't use a map, just take a turning to the right here .... and there a turn to the left .... to the right again without a plan .... and then wondering which is the right direction to go .... what do you really want to do?

Consider now the animals of this world .... those that migrate from place to place .... How would it feel if you were to wake one day and suddenly feel that feeling that tells you .... as sure as you can be, that it is time to do something different .... time to fly south .... time to swim north .... to cross the ocean .... or the mountains .... the feeling that the whales feel .... that the snow geese feel .... that the king salmon feels .... that the wildebeest feel.

I wonder how it would feel to know something without knowing why .... know something deep down .... and be so sure that you know .... what is wanted .... what is needed .... in the way that a small child knows when it needs to drink .... but still does not know what thirsty means .... a craving   .... perhaps a desire .... wanting .... whenever our mind can picture the kind of meal that we crave.

You watch people in a restaurant .... looking through the menu .... allowing their mind to imagine the texture of this food or the taste of that .... until they find one that tastes perfect to the mind .... like trying on clothes to see if they suit .... or possible futures .... imagining the time and the place .... that tastes .... feels .... looks and sounds just right .... yes, that's it .... everything in imagination .... just fine .... experiencing that future feeling of satisfaction when everything is just fine .... and you finally have what is needed .... and have done all that is required to have that way of being you .... to hold that wonderful feeling .... and to know that there is no need to wonder .... no need to wander any longer .... to know what direction to take and to enjoy that knowing and going there when you want to from now on .... like a homing pigeon that somehow seems to know which way there .... back to where it belongs .... it gets its bearings .... knows which way to go and it goes there to where it needs to be to feel comfortable and happy .... where it needs to be.

And I am reminded too of the man who rode a bicycle each and every day to his work and then back home in the evening .... a machine that he had had for many years .... a gift from someone who loved him .... someone who was happy to make him happy. He was so delighted with that bike .... he cleaned it and polished it .... oiled it and made certain that every small part was kept in good condition. The bicycle served him well .... carrying him so many hundreds of miles .... to work and even on holidays .... carrying too all of his camping equipment .... and all that he needed to enjoy the experience without concern that he would not have what was needed.

He called one day at a shop in town to buy a new tyre for his tried and tested steed .... and it was then that he saw the new model .... a bicycle with all of the newest features .... deraillier gears .... sports handlebars .... a drinks container that he could drink from as he rode .... the paint was so bright and so shiny .... and he wondered how it would be to ride that bike .... to own that bike .... after all, the one he had was old .... and he knew it so well .... all of its scratches .... all of its little faults .... things that needed to be attended to, like the tyre that was now worn .... and there was no desire .... no feeling of excitement .... at what was known .... so familiar .... and so he determined right there and then that that bicycle would be his .... that he would save all of his money and would have for himself that new and exciting machine.

He continued to ride his old bike .... now imagining himself on that new machine .... longing for the day when he would achieve his goal and own that new machine .... but he neglected his old bike that had carried him through .... and carried him still .... did not bother to clean it or to look after it any more .... as he dreamed only of that machine that would be his.

Then came the day when he realized that dream .... that new bike was his, and he abandoned his old and faithful machine .... leaving it to rust and decay in the garden shed of his parents' home .... and he rode that bike in all its splendour .... others admired it and wanted it too .... and then one day it was taken away .... stolen .... and he was so sad .... that attractive machine .... that so many others admired and desired .... had been taken by another .... never to be seen again.

He went back to that old and faithful machine .... and soon discovered that it had been there all the time .... there when he needed it .... ready to begin again .... and not to complain or let him down .... and he never ever did need to drink whilst riding along .... some attention now needed .... and a coat of paint can be so easily applied .... even as the imagination can choose to allow that look or this look to seem perfect or not .... and when that knot is tied .... will that knot be the one that will slip .... or not ....?

And I know that you too will choose that which is right for you to do .... aware of what is true and that which is durable .... that will be there whenever you need the comfort and the stability of something comfortable .... like a jumper or a pair of shoes that fits just so .... aware of the comfort .... and aware that you do not need to know how it is comfortable .... it does not concern you .... it is just comfortable .... as your own unconscious mind is allowed now to do those things .... that are the right things for you .... as you trust even more than ever before that part of you which takes care of your best interests .... to your highest good.

Roger P. Allen

The Art Collection

Metaphor for smoking & substance abuse etc.

I am reminded of a man whom I new many years ago, named Henry, who was very interested in art. He didn't have much money, but he worked hard and saved what he could to put together a very fine collection of works of art of which he was justifiably proud.

He consulted an acquaintance of his, an acknowledged expert, as to the best way of looking after his collection of fine porcelain and china. The acquaintance sold him a special substance, which he had formulated, with precise instructions as to the manner and the frequency with which it should be used. He told Henry that, if he used it regularly, then he would have no need to worry and that he could just relax, happy in the knowledge that he was doing the best he could to preserve his collection of fine works.

Henry paid the money and, throughout the years, he cleaned and lavished attention on his valued collection, always ensuring that he purchased a good supply of the compound, feeling relaxed with the thought and the idea that he was doing the best that he could to ensure the well being of his works of art.

He failed to notice the fact that he always seemed to have a dull throbbing headache. The skin on his hands became reddened and sore, his fingernails became brittle and unsightly, and nothing seemed to make it better. He was unaware of the pungent smell that had become part of his person. It clung to his clothes and his hair. At least he had his collection of fine works of art.

It was a few years before he managed to put aside enough money to take the holiday that he had planned for so long. Before he left, he asked a very good friend of his to look after his collection while he was away. He gave precise instructions as to how the art treasures should be cleaned and attended to, using the special compound that was so important to him for his peace of mind. The friend promised to do as Henry asked, even though the smell of the compound was disgusting, and it so easily stained his hands and clothing.

Henry went on his holiday and was amazed to discover that after just a few days the headaches and the pains, the reddened and sore hands, cleared up and he felt so much better and more alive than he had felt for such a long time.

Imagine how he felt on his return when he found that his friend was unwell, suffering as he had done. And the smell now so apparent upon him was so disgusting. He quickly deduced that the compound that he had relied on so much for peace of mind was the problem, and a professional analysis established that it was full of poisonous and toxic chemicals. That very day Henry destroyed his whole stock of the compound, and he knew that his health was worth more than any possession no matter how valuable or rare. Henry sought further advice from the most respected experts in their field as to alternatives to meeting his responsibility of caring for his all-important works of art, in a beneficial and healthy manner.

To his surprise, the answer was simple and inexpensive, and it had been there in front of him all the time: simple solutions of mild and appropriate cleaning materials would achieve exactly the results that he desired. His works of art would be cleaned and cared for in the most natural way that would prove healthy and beneficial.

The manufacturer of the compound would continue to produce and sell his lethal poison without regard or pity for those who would suffer from his irresponsible and mercenary actions, but Henry had made the decision to take responsibility for his own life and his own health. No longer would he rely on the advice of others whose best interests were not Henry's. He had accepted the evidence as it was, relying on his own judgment and his own ability, not knowing or needing to know how his own inner mind knew what to do for him, and I wonder now if you will not now allow your own wise inner advisor to do those things needed for you?.... and you will, will you not?

(Go to Stop Smoking or whichever script is appropriate.)

The above metaphor lends itself to so many applications. I wonder how many you will find it useful for?

Anchors

An anchor is simply a stimulus which initiates a response, in the same way that you will experience some anxiety perhaps whilst in the waiting room of your dentist, or that funny feeling you get when you see a police car in your rear view mirror, and that response of glancing at the speedometer.

Then, of course, there is the subconscious stimulus that results in a response of lighting up a cigarette, after a meal, on the telephone, with a drink, etc. Clearly the response can be a pleasant one, such as the pleasure that we feel when we hear the voice of a loved one; a picture perhaps or a word that stimulates a warm glow of remembrance of a special event or person - the response that is experienced when a favourite treat is mentioned such as a Black Forest gateau, but then that is my Achilles heel; I wonder what is yours?

These can be termed "conditional responses", the stimulus being associated with a particular event or circumstance, but the important thing for us here is that a response can be controlled if we are able to marry a particular event or stimulus to a desired response or reaction.

A stimulus can be any one of many events, be it taste, feel, colour, hearing or smell. A most useful explanation is the following extract from **Neuro-Linguistic Programming, Vol 1**:

"Anchoring is in many ways simply the user-oriented version of the stimulus response concept in behavioristic models. There are however, some major differences between the two. These include:

> *1) Anchors do not need to be conditioned over long periods of time in order to be experienced. That kind of conditioning undoubtedly will contribute to the establishment of the anchor, but it is often the initial experience that establishes the anchor most firmly. Anchors then promote the use of single trial learning.*

2)   *The association between the anchor and the response need not be directly reinforced by any immediate outcome resulting from the association in order to be established. That is, anchors or associations will become established without direct rewards or reinforcement for the association. Reinforcement, like conditioning, will contribute to the establishment of an anchor, but is not required.*

3)   *Internal experience (i.e. cognitive behaviour) is considered to be as significant, behaviourally, as the overt measurable responses; in other words NLP (Neuro-Linguistic Programming) asserts that an internal dialogue, picture or feeling constitutes as much of a response as the salivation of Pavlov's dogs."*

Dilts, Grinder, Bandler, Delozier, 1980.

The following script for Nail Biting can be regarded as a generic habit script using anchoring techniques. It will not need great leaps of imagination to see how this format can be used for so many problems by simple substitution of the symptomatic response that is undesirable.

Nail Biting

And now as you relax even deeper, listening to the sound of my voice .... each word that I speak Here can be a signal for you to go deeper still as you rest, so comfortable and quiet There. I wonder if you can really be aware now of how much more comfortable you can become .... as you begin now to sense in some safe and agreeable way .... a gentle connection between your mind and your body that has no part to play here .... all that is required is that you continue to allow those comfortable hypnotic sensation .... heaviness of arms .... of legs .... comfortably heavy .... to deepen even more .... as your whole body relaxes .... all tension just draining away .... and you can turn inward now .... deep inside to where that part of you that is all-knowing .... creative and perfect .... is ready now to do its best work for you .... to help you make those changes that you want to make .... that you can make and will make.

That's good *(client's name)*; now I would like you to allow your subconscious to take you back in time .... back to a time when you were really confident in your ability to take control and to be in control .... a memory of yours .... pleasant and reassuring .... when you really did feel good .... powerful .... assertive .... and allow that experience to develop and those good feelings to expand .... and when you are fully experiencing that event .... I want you to allow your subconscious to lift the pointing finger of your right hand..... *(ideomotor response)*. If you experience any difficulty in recalling a memory that is appropriate, then that's fine .... you can allow your subconscious to create a scene where you are confident and in total control .... go ahead now ....

(Watch for responses including skin tone and breathing as well as ideomotor response.)

(Now tell the client that you are going to touch them several times on the shoulder or arm. Then gently but firmly grasp the shoulder or arm of the client and continue to maintain the pressure for about 10 to 15 seconds to establish the anchor.)

That's good, you are doing this very well .... and now I want you to allow that scene to fade and your mind to become as before, calm and quiet. Now I would like you to allow your subconscious mind to show you a scene .... in the future at one of the next times when you would bite your nails .... your hands staying where they are now comfortably in your lap There..... having no part to play Here. .... Allow that scene and that experience to develop and become real .... those feelings to expand and grow .... and you can allow your subconscious to let me know when that is done .... as that pointing finger on your right hand can lift. *(Touch finger.)*

(Watch for responses including skin tone and breathing as well as ideomotor response. Now again grasp firmly the shoulder or arm of the client as exactly before and continue for about 10 to 15 seconds to "fire" the anchor.)

That's fine .... you really are doing this well .... and I wonder now just how you feel about biting your nails .... how you will find it so easy to not do that anymore .... remembering how unpleasant and how bad it made you feel because now you know what you are not going to do .... and how to remind yourself with an irresistible response .... reaching deep into the subconscious of your mind, that you will never ever be able to do that again in that way or at all .... because if you do then you will be doing it on purpose .... and that's a different matter entirely .... it all belongs to you.

Sexual Problems:

Impotence And Inorgasmia

I wonder if you are really aware of those things that are done automatically .... those instinctive things that the body can do for you that need not be learned .... but have been learned in some special way .... like the new-born babe who knows just how to suckle exactly .... and becomes aware of the pleasure that can be from those parts which are sexual .... and in the same way can do those things that you want to do and those things that you want to happen.

Now you have come here because you want to know that you do know how to have those thing happen .... and experience those sensations and pleasures in that special way .... so I would like you now to listen carefully to what I am going to say .... and to what happens to you .... sensations and pleasures that are natural and desirable .... that you can enjoy and continue to enjoy as you begin to know even more than before that you really have known all along how to respond and to never forget that responding.

As you concentrate fully now on my voice and on those sexual sensual parts of you .... where sensations are even now beginning to stir .... I want you to know that there are things that you can think .... images that you can create that can cause those sensations to occur and those physical changes to occur .... thoughts and images that perhaps you would consider inappropriate .... quite indecent perhaps .... but which can stimulate the imagination .... creating scenes for you within the privacy of your own imagination .... erotic and sensual thoughts .... of emotions and sensations .... that will arouse that natural and pleasurable instinctive subconscious reaction to a special wonderful need that is the most natural and beautiful part of our human creation.

You can allow these thoughts to grow..... utilize these feelings that are yours .... fantasies provided for you by that part of you which does know just how to do those things for you .... uninhibited and free of conscious restraint .... and it can enjoy .... as you enjoy allowing those thoughts and images to continue naked and unashamed .... and allowing you now to experience those sensations there .... that touching glow of pleasure .... as you begin to know what a difference that difference can make when they begin to touch .... to caress .... and then to enter in that gentle .... special .... deep penetrating way .... gently moving to establish a bond and a remembrance that will be there to enjoy as that time comes .... coming together .... and you will come to know that it really is okay to experience in that way .... to give and to receive that special and private gift .... and you can know that when you leave here today that you can experience that softening and that moistening .... that firm feeling that becomes larger and harder to know just how it begins .... as you discover even more than before just how easy it can be to know how that which works for you .... time after time again .... whenever you want or need to .... it all belongs to you.

When you leave here today .... intensely aware that you do know how to do those things .... I would caution you that it can be awkward if you know too well and too often .... you could become excited and aroused all of the time .... just imagine how it would be to be that way .... so full of wanting .... so full of firm desire that it could be so moist .... so hard to contain .... and others may notice too how easy it can be to remember to be ready .... so awkward .... it could be embarrassing.

Taking Responsibility

Metaphor and suggestion for determining what is important:

As you rest quietly there, aware now of that gentle connection between your mind and your perfect inner self .... that part of you that has all those capacities .... knowledge and abilities to solve those problems that are causing you pain .... to create for you so many alternatives that are positive and beneficial to your highest good .... I am reminded of a client of mine who came to see me for help with a problem that he had at work.

Now John had a very good job with an insurance company, and he had a lot of colleagues working with him whom he regarded as friends .... people he would often socialise with and who came to dinner parties at his home .... he had a very good social life indeed.

John was very good at his job and often he would be able to help others with his knowledge and his enthusiasm. Because he worked with people that he regarded as friends, he felt very much that he had a duty to help them in any way that he could. He would sort the problems of his friends because he had confidence in his own abilities and thought that he could do it so much better than they.

He spent a great deal of his time and energy putting the mistakes and omissions of others to rights, ensuring in this way that they would not suffer from their lack of ability and enthusiasm, and lose for the company valuable business. He defended their mistakes and even covered up for them using his own time and energy to visit clients on their behalf to ensure that contracts were finalised.

His friends did very well by him. He worked long hours and took on the stress and the pressure in making absolutely sure that he did all he could to help them. After all, these people were his friends, and true friends will always make sacrifices for those whom they care about.

He failed to take much notice at first of the growing and constant headaches, the tiredness and of the fact that he had become so short-tempered, snapping at his wife and children for no good reason.

He was not too much concerned that the sexual interest in his marriage was now almost non-existent and that his family life seemed to be sliding down a long and slippery slope of constant rows and upsets. His smile had gone, his energy spent and he spent longer and longer hours at the office struggling to complete the immense workload that he had forgotten almost entirely was not his, but that of others.

I wonder if you can imagine his feelings when one day he was called into his superior's office, to be told that a review of personal performance figures had shown that he was producing less business and was now below the average of the rest of the people in his department? He was told that, because of the decline in his performance, the promotion that he had been expecting would not be his, that his performance would be monitored and reviewed on a weekly basis and that he was at risk of losing his position if his performance did not improve.

He went back to his desk, very upset and confused. After all, he knew his job so well and had worked harder and longer than anyone else in the office.

He then discovered that the friend whom he had helped most, whom he had carried and covered for, whose mistakes he had rectified, was the one who had received the promotion that was to be his.

It took a very true and special friend to tell him the truth, and it was with great sadness that he eventually came to the realisation that, in taking on the responsibilities for the lives and the problems of those whom he considered his friends, he had neglected to his own detriment the responsibility that was his, the responsibility for his own health and happiness and for his own wife and children, the responsibility to take for himself the time to ensure the quality of life that was his by right. He took a decision to accept the responsibility that was his, to do that which was beneficial and right for him and for those he loved and cared for.

He had some leave to come and made a decision to take himself and his wife and children away on holiday, and for two glorious weeks devoted all of his energies to putting back that which had been lost. As if by magic, the headaches and the lack-lustre feelings just dissolved away as he involved himself once again with the important and valuable things of life. He relaxed, as you are now so very relaxed, and rediscovered the pleasure of a loving wife and the joys of children .... it did not take long for him to realise the truth, and to recognise that he had become obsessed with taking on the responsibilities of others.

He resolved to take care of the most important elements of his life, his wife and family and himself .... Those who loved him and whom he loved and cared for were where his true responsibilities lay.

When he returned after his holiday, I wonder if you can imagine his feelings to discover that the office was in a state of chaos? His colleagues made it plain to him that they felt that he had let them down by going away and leaving then so much work to do.

It was with great deliberation that he addressed the entire staff that day. He explained to them that he would no longer be prepared to take on their workload and that they would have to accept for themselves the responsibility that was theirs for their own performance. He made plain that he would not interfere in that responsibility but that, if his advice was required, he would be pleased to give the benefit of his experience, but that decisions taken would have to be their own. He spoke of how they would all need to accept their own responsibility for their own life, no more or no less than he was for his; that they were all entitled, as was he, to the rewards for their own efforts and diligence, and not that for which they had been prepared to see him make all that effort, on their behalf.

It didn't take long for the office to fall in line with these new rules and very soon John was back on top where he belonged. He no longer took on any responsibility other than that which was his, and his colleagues soon realised that, with just a bit more effort, they too could do well. They learned to accept the advice that John would give, but also that they needed to ask for that advice and then to accept the responsibility for the decision that needed to be made. Perhaps, too, a lesson was learned that gifts given should be appreciated and treasured, and that kindness improves with the giving.

Experience can be a bitter pill to swallow, as the realisation dawns that even friends will happily allow their responsibilities to be shouldered by another, while they reap the benefit of labour and effort that is not theirs; perhaps you can wonder too that the time given was so greedily taken and then so casually acknowledged.

I know that you will take the time to give to yourself that which you are entitled to, time to care for you, not in an egotistical way, but in a way that will mean that you make those decisions which are right for you and for those whom you love and care for. You accept now, without reservation or pause, the responsibility that can only be yours, and allow others the freedom to choose what is right for them. You wish, for all those around you, the same good feelings of freedom and of confidence in your own abilities and capacities that you enjoy, as you establish yourself as your own person, that person whom you like and respect, a confidant of your own wise inner advisor as you allow that wonderful feeling of oneness with yourself to expand and cocoon you now with its soothing light of beneficial calm and positivity. Now you are your own person .... are you not?

(Await response and go to trance termination).

Roger P. Allen

Pleasure Returned

Metaphor and suggestion for premature ejaculation.

I wonder if you have ever had that pleasure of looking around a beautiful garden .... and wonder just how you can best appreciate the wonders that are there .... the carefully planted borders .... the colours and the variety of plants all creating a harmony, and then a complementary variance .... blooms each in their time throughout the whole of the four seasons .... You can see those who will look at all that is there .... darting from this plant to that shrub, so full of wonder that they really cannot decide which to look at .... which to savour and appreciate first .... there is so much to enjoy .... so much to savour .... the shouts of joyous discovery .... look at this .... look at that .... isn't it lovely .... beautiful .... then to rush on to the next .... so much beauty .... so much colour .... confusing and confounding .... the wanting to see it all .... Now .... enjoy it all .... Now .... miss nothing .... have it all .... so they rush without giving time to express the real appreciation in a controlled and considered manner.

There are those who cultivate these delights .... tilling the soil and ensuring that what is offered is of ultimate beauty .... ensuring that the colour and the variety is ever there .... waiting for that time when the garden is open .... the public allowed in .... its pleasures to be enjoyed .... Those who take the time .... who make available to us the pleasures that will be provided with love and with gentle care .... can watch as those who would enjoy, take their pleasure .... those who take more time .... relaxing and experiencing as they look at each and every petal .... every leaf .... every branch .... so many varieties .... savouring the essence of natural joy in those things which are as nature intended .... will also take the time to seek out the gardener .... the provider of all of this pleasure .... this sensual delight .... and extend to that person who has given so much of themselves .... the thanks and appreciation which are also to be enjoyed .... then giving and receiving so much more as that interest .... that gentle consideration is rewarded with personal attention and direction to the hidden delights .... the subtle pleasures .... extending the time of pleasure with pleasurable anticipation .... taking the time now to enjoy each step .... each movement, each new experience..... and learning more of that gardener's pleasure in what is provided there .... pausing to allow

48

time to explore even more than before those areas of pleasure that are hidden from those who rush by .... even trampled and crushed underfoot .... murmurings of pleasure .... appreciation of that beauty and that care .... reverence and respect .... allowing the beauty to embrace and enfold .... that takes them into another quiet and tranquil experience away from the hurry and scurry of those who will see only what is there for them .... too excited .... too uncontrolled to share .... and it can be so satisfying knowing that when all is done .... all is appreciated and that appreciation expressed .... that pleasure returned and shared .... that it really is okay to let go in that way .... letting that feeling grow, allowing those emotions to explode in a couplet of delight .... then to tarry a while .... knowing that they really can .... and can return again and again .... and each time more is discovered .... the gardener becomes a trusted and beloved companion .... each visit a sharing experience as knowledge grows and each of those pleasures can become something that happens time after time as your subconscious mind finds new and more exciting .... pleasurable ways for you .... with an understanding of those things which are there all of the time .... hidden within the realms of your higher mind .... now shown in a wonderful clarity to you as you learn even more about those things that are done for you in that way .... automatically.

So now you can relax deeper now .... in communion with that special and all-knowing part of your perfect mind .... that does know how .... and then the next time that you enter into that garden .... perhaps to plant the seeds .... that sown with love will blossom and bloom .... I am sure that you will too take the time to prepare the richness of the soil and give appropriate consideration for the miracle that is yours to enjoy .... and I know too that you will remember to recognize that time when the garden is in bloom and the blossoms open .... the soil moist and receptive .... as the bees know that time, to then allow that conclusion .... that pollination .... that climax to come .... it's completely up to you to enjoy yourself .... or to enjoy yourself giving enjoyment and pleasure .... in return as you take your time .... to pause .... to allow that your love .... your appreciation be appreciated too .... and you will .... will you not?

Pain Management:

Switches For Pain

Now, before you wake up completely, I would like you to just close your eyes again and allow that drifting down again, entering again that place of calm relaxation, because there was a young boy on TV not long ago, who had learned to control all of his pain. He described the steps that he went down in his mind, one at a time down those steps, until he found this hall at the bottom, like a long tunnel, and all along this tunnel on both side were many different switches and switchboxes, all clearly labelled. One for the right hand, one for the left, one for each leg, a switch for every part of the body, and he could see clearly the wires that carried the sensations from one place to another, all going through those switches.

All he needed to do here was to reach up in his mind and turn off the switches that he wanted to, and then he could feel nothing at all, no sensation could get through from there, because he had turned off the appropriate switches there.

He used his mind's abilities differently from the man who simply made his body numb. He didn't know how he did it exactly. All he knew was, he relaxed and disconnected from the rest, moved his mind away from his body, moved it outside somewhere else, where he could watch and listen, but drift off somewhere else entirely. It really doesn't matter how you tell your subconscious what to do, or how your unconscious does it for you. The only thing of importance is that you know you can lose sensations as easily as closing your eyes, and drifting down within where something unknown happens that allows you to disconnect, that allows that numbness to occur, and then a drifting back upwards now, towards the surface, and slowly opening the eyes as wakeful awareness returns with a comfortable continuation of that feeling of safe, secure relaxation and an ability to forget an arm, or anything at all, with no need to pay attention to things that are just fine, that somebody else can take care of for a while, while you drift in your mind and then return when it is time to enjoy that comfortable drifting upwards where the eyes open and wakeful awareness returns completely .... NOW.

The Dentist

Now as you sit comfortably there with your eyes closed .... comfortable and aware that you are here because you want to learn to use your own subconscious abilities to help you to eliminate that discomfort you experience .... that anxiety .... when you visit your dentist. And so .... as you begin to relax and to drift down into trance .... deeper now .... into a deep trance state .... I want you to take your time .... not go too quickly .... yet .... because there are some things that you need to first understand .... so please listen carefully now.

First you need to understand that you already have the ability to lose an arm .... or a hand .... to become totally unaware of just where that arm is positioned .... or the fingers .... and you do have an ability to be unconcerned about exactly where that ear or thumb went .... or that hand .... that leg .... or your entire body .... which may seem to require too much effort to pay attention to at times. Because you do have an ability .... a subconscious ability you can learn to use .... an ability to turn off the sensation in an arm .... a leg .... or even your face .... your jaw .... your gum .... in fact any place.

And once you discover how it feels to feel nothing at all .... whenever you want or need that to occur .... then you can create a comfortable, numb feeling any time .... anywhere that is useful for you.

And I don't know if your unconscious mind can allow you to discover that numb feeling in the right hand .... or a finger of the left hand first .... a tiny area of numbness .... a comfortable tickly feeling .... a heavy .... enveloping numbness .... that seems to spread within time .... over the back of the hand .... covering that hand .... or any part of you that you direct your attention to .... it just fades away .... but you don't know how it feels to feel that something that is not there .... so I would like you to just reach over to that numb, comfortable area .... that numb, comfortable hand .... now .... touch it .... and feel that touching .... as you begin to pinch yourself there .... a sensation that you may be aware of at first .... but as you continue to pinch yourself .... something special happens here .... you begin to experience and discover that there are times when you feel nothing at all there .... that sensation just seems to fade away .... as you learn how to allow your subconscious mind to do that for you .... to turn off those sensations .... and as that ability grows and you become more aware .... that you really do know how .... to really turn off that part .... really know how to switch off those sensations and allow that pain and discomfort to just disappear from that hand .... or from anywhere .... your other hand can return to its resting position .... and you can drift up now towards the surface of wakeful awareness .... so go ahead now as you relax .... and discover how to let go .... and to re-experience that numbness more and more clearly .... and so you can drift up .... and then back down, as you learn even more about your own ability .... in your own time .... in your own way .... you can practise this self-learning .... this ability to do that for you at any time .... at any place.

(Give the client time to practise this technique a few times, and then continue.....)

Now (*client's name*), with your eyes closed .... you can relax more deeply than before .... aware of that new learning .... that new ability to switch off that discomfort .... You can visualize now as vividly as you can .... see yourself at your next visit to your dentist .... please notice now how calm you are feeling as you check in at the desk .... in plenty of time for your appointment.

You now sit in the waiting area .... feeling calm and unconcerned .... confident in your ability to control those sensations .... you smile at others who are waiting with you .... pleased to be able to allow your own calm and confident manner to soothe the minds of others .... as they wait to be called.

As you wait there, you practise again your ability to turn off that sensation there .... and experience now that numbness .... as the sensation in your gums just fades .... that numbness spreading .... just as if you had been given a shot of local anaesthetic .... that woolly, thick feeling of no feeling at all .... and you relax experiencing a total inner calm.

When your turn comes to be called for your appointment .... you take a long deep breath .... and as you expel all the air from your lungs .... you breathe out anxiety .... fear .... and then breathe in calm .... confidence .... tranquillity.

As you sit in the dentist's chair .... you will experience a comfortable sensation as calm fills your mind .... as you relax .... concentrating now on that switch that will allow you to experience that sensation of no sensation .... as your dentist gently and carefully begins the work that is needed to be done.

If he needs to give you anaesthesia, you will be calm and comfortable .... but I really do not want you to giggle when you experience that tickle .... and may I mention too that I wouldn't want you to drift off too deeply into a trance too quickly as the sound of the drill and the gentle soothing vibrations relax you and calm you .... you will be pleasurably surprised at how calm and relaxed you will become as your dentist .... appreciating your necessary co-operation .... completes his work easily .... skillfully .... you will enjoy being that person who relaxes in that chair and allows your subconscious to utilize that special ability that you have learned .... looking forward to your regular check-ups .... no longer bothered or concerned as you now take control of that fear .... and unlearn that fear .... seeing it now for exactly what it was .... no longer imagining in that way that tells you that there are things to fear here .... as your subconscious mind takes care of you .... takes care of those thoughts those feelings automatically .... aware that you can trust you to be okay, with no need to pay attention to things that are just fine .... things that somebody else can just take care of .... and it doesn't really matter exactly how you tell your subconscious mind what to do or how your subconscious mind does it for you .... the only thing of importance is that you know that you can lose those sensations .... those discomforts .... just as easily as closing your eyes .... while you drift in your mind and then return when it is time .... back to wakeful awareness .... quite completely now.

Therapy Strategies:

Six-Step Reframe

Basic Steps:

1. Identify the habit or compulsive pattern of behaviour [X] to be changed.

2. Establish communication with that part that has been responsible for [X].

3. Suggest that behaviour [X] be separated from the positive intervention of the part responsible for [X]: in other words, [X] has had pay-offs or benefits for the client.

4. Suggest that the client generate new behaviours that provide the needed pay-offs.

5. Do an "ecological check". Are the alternative patterns of behaviour acceptable to all parts of the person ?

6. Future pace. Check out the alternative patterns of behaviour within relevant future contexts.

Technique:

Take a few deep breaths now, and make yourself comfortable, relaxing deeper with each easy breath that you take, and take a few moments to concentrate on that *(insert habit or behaviour)* that you wish to change, but something is stopping you.

Now that you know that changing this habit is important to you, I would like you to know that I have so often found that the part which is preventing you from making the change you want to make is an unconscious part of you.

If that is the case here, I would like to ask that part of you to now make itself known, in some safe way, to your unconscious mind. Please take a few moments of time to go into your own inner mind -

wherever you have to go - and become aware of the part of you which, in the past, has been responsible for *(insert habit or behaviour)*.

Now I don't know exactly how you will experience that part of you which has been responsible for *(insert habit or behaviour)* .... It may be a familiar type of experience, or a unique one .... It may be something you see in your mind's eye: it can be any visual image at all .... For example, you may see a face or an object, or the experience of that inner part of you may be auditory .... such as a voice - perhaps your own, or someone else's - or some other sound .... Your experience of that part of you may be a feeling of some kind.

Please go into your own inner mind now .... With respect I ask that part of you to allow itself to be experienced in some kind of safe comfortable way by your consciousness .... If you do not become aware of any particular experience which can be identified as an awareness that is responsible, ... then that is fine, ... please proceed with the understanding that your subconscious may not be just comfortable with your experiencing what I have suggested, and that's all right .... If you are experiencing that part of you which is responsible for *(insert habit or behaviour)*, I would like now to thank that part for communicating, and to suggest that you might also wish to thank that part.

I want now to let the part of you responsible for *(insert habit or behaviour)* in the past know that it has my respect .... That part is obviously very powerful, because even though you have wanted to make this change in the past, you haven't been able to do so. Therefore I understand that this part of you responsible for your problem will change it only when it is ready to do so.

I would now like to suggest to you that, in some kind of way, *(insert habit or behaviour)* has had benefits or pay-offs for you in the past, that you have in some way gained an advantage .... I understand that the actual experience or behaviour of that part has caused negative or unhealthy consequences for you, but I am suggesting that you now reframe your understanding of it to realise that the intention of that part of you has been to help you or benefit you. Now take a few moments of time to go into your own inner mind and become aware of what the pay-offs or benefits of *(insert habit or behaviour)* have been for you.

Has *(insert habit or behaviour)* helped get something that some part of you has desired *(give example of possible pay-off)*. .... Has it helped you avoid something that would be uncomfortable or painful *(possible example)*? .... I am asking you again to assume that *(insert behaviour or habit)* has continued up to now because it has helped you or benefited you in some way. So *(client's name)*, please become aware, if it is safe and comfortable enough to have this awareness, of how *(insert habit or behaviour)* has helped you.

Now, keeping the pay-off or pay-offs in mind, ... I would like to suggest that available to you are alternative patterns of behaviour, ... of experiencing, ... or perception, that can provide whatever benefits or pay-offs *[insert behaviour or habit]* you had in the past. However, these new patterns of behaviour would be healthier and perhaps even more satisfying to you. .... Now take some moments of time and go into your mind again.

Tap into the creative resources of your mind and allow it to generate for you alternative patterns of behaviour that you can substitute for *(insert habit or behaviour)*, that will give you the same pay-offs as *(insert habit or behaviour)*, but be healthier for you.

Now that you have constructed alternative patterns of behaviour, the next step is to check with that part of you that was responsible for *(insert habit or behaviour)*, as well as all the other parts of you, that they will be comfortable and satisfied with the new alternatives.

Would you go into your mind again and make sure that all the new alternatives seem all right, ... sound all right .... and feel all right to that part of you that was responsible for *(insert habit or behaviour)*, and to all parts of you.

If you receive a "no" signal, or in any way experience incongruence from any part of you - for example irritability or increase in tension - in response to your new alternative or alternatives, then it is necessary that you return to a prior step of reframing. You may need to go back and allow your creative part to generate a new alternative or alternatives. Or you may have to go back even further to identify and take into account some benefit or pay-off that you were not aware of before. If your new alternatives are okay, then I would like you to go back into your inner mind to take part in an exercise called "future pacing".

Please now go into your inner mind again and imagine yourself in the future on occasions when you would have, in the past, indulged in *(insert habit or behaviour)*. Imagine yourself in these future contexts with the ability to use these new alternative patterns of behaviour that you have just become aware of.

Imagine yourself in these future contexts with these alternative patterns. If you experience significant difficulty, it may be necessary for you to generate more suitable alternatives. When you have completed generating for yourself suitable alternatives which are beneficial and healthy, and have imagined successfully future contexts with alternative patterns of behaviour, then you have completed the process of reframing. I would suggest now that you thank your subconscious mind for communicating in that way, and I would like to express my appreciation for the healthy work that you have just completed and extend my thanks for the valuable communication.

Use suggestion for amnesia. Go to trance termination and do not discuss session content with client before he/she leaves.

Original concept : Bandler/Grinder, *Reframing*, 1982

Parts Therapy

Generic

1. Explain the concept to the client before inducing hypnosis. The procedure is not dependent upon this explanation, but will serve to allay any problems alluding to "Multiple Personality"

2. Induce hypnosis using your choice of induction and deepener.

3. Tell the client:
   "You can speak to me now but you will not wake. .... I am now going to speak directly to your subconscious mind .... and I want to speak specifically to that part which is responsible for *(detail problem)* .... Are you the part of *(client's name)* that is responsible for this problem *(detail problem)*? .... Please answer 'yes' or 'no'."

4. Having received a positive response, thank the part for coming forward:
   "Thank you for coming forward today and speaking with me .... please tell me your name .... are you male or female?"

5. Ask how old the whole person was when the part first appeared .... encourage dissociation by proper use of pronouns.
   "How old was *(client's name)* when you first appeared?" *(Note: The ego state is usually "young", so address it in simple language).*

6. "Tell me *(name of part)* what was happening to *(client's name)* that caused you to first appear?" *(Elicit elaboration of those events).*

7. Now attempt to define the part's goal:
   "So, you appeared in order to *(punish, comfort, etc.)* .... Is that true?"

8. Comment on the value of the goal and its appropriateness. Redefine it in positive terms.

9. Offer an alternative and more appropriate method of obtaining these goals; .... ask for the part's co-operation in trying out these new methods for just one week to see how they work out.

10. Thank the part for its co-operation and assure it that you will check progress with it at the next session:
"Thank you for coming forward to speak to me today, and for the co-operation that you have shown. I would like to ask if there is any other part that objects to this arrangement? *(Provided there is a negative response:)* You may return now from where you came .... I will speak with you at our next session."

11. Trance termination:
"When I complete a count of three, the whole person that is *(client's name)* will open his/her eyes and return to fully-awake awareness .... remembering everything of this session that can be handled comfortably."

12. Use distraction to discourage rationalization of the session content; .... terminate session as quickly as is respectfully possible.

Strategy For Past-Life Recall
(P.L.R.)

Before embarking on a past-life recall, I explain carefully to the client the powers of the imagination and the nature of memory. It is important that the client is aware of the possibility that memories recalled may be simply those of watching a film or reading a book, or even just an imagined event. The subconscious memory does not differentiate and will accept all memory as actuality. What the client chooses to accept as truth must be left entirely to them. Whether or not you, the therapist, accept or deny the truth of the events occurring is of no consequence).

Carry out a lengthy induction:

Deepening with imagery:

"Now I would like you to imagine yourself in a place that will provide for you feelings of peace and comfort .... security .... tranquillity .... It may be winter, summer, ... spring or autumn .... there may be trees .... mountains .... water .... lush green meadows .... or perhaps a beach with the waves rolling in from the ocean .... whichever place you choose will have great peace and harmony, and you feel totally safe and secure here .... and as you become more and more involved with this place that you have chosen, you can relax even deeper than before .... relaxing .... releasing .... just letting go completely.

This is your own private and secret place, and you are aware that this place is your own haven deep inside where only peace and harmony abide .... and you can go so much deeper now .... turning inward to your innermost self .... where all knowledge and all memories are kept safe for you .... some easily accessible .... others hidden deep where they can not be so easily recalled .... but they are there .... each and every one .... never forgotten from so far back in this life and a time when this life was not yet begun .... memories that have shaped and moulded your unique and special personality .... and as you go deep inside now .... you can begin to experience a gentle connection with that special part of you which holds those memories that you now wish to explore and to re-experience .... that part now makes itself known to you in some special and safe way that you can recognize easily .... Tell me *(client's name)*, do you have any special or strange feelings or sensations? *(Wait for response)* .... *(When your client reports any strange or unusual sensation, sound or image, continue)*.

Okay, that's good .... now let that feeling or experience grow stronger as you go deeper inside to connect more fully with that part of you. .... Now I am going to speak directly to your subconscious mind, and I am going to ask your subconscious for permission to conduct a past-life recall .... I want your subconscious to give me the answer .... please do not do anything at all .... just continue to enjoy the peace and comfort of this place that you have chosen.

(The use of ideomotor response can be utilized at this juncture .... see script on page 21.)

I am now going to touch your forehead and ask the question. My words go directly into your subconscious and the answer, either 'yes' or 'no', will come directly from that part of you. Please do not involve yourself at all as your subconscious mind provides the answer to my question. *(Touch centre of forehead with finger.)*

Am I speaking to that part of *(client's name)* which is able to give me permission to conduct a past-life recall .... answer 'yes' or 'no' .... *(Wait for response. If answer is 'yes' you can proceed)*. Thank you, subconscious mind, for communicating with me .... I have been asked by *(client's name)* to help him/her to go back to that time, before this life, to a previous existence .... Do I have your permission to do this and your help in this? Answer 'yes' or 'no'.

(Await response. If response is 'yes', then continue).

Thank you, subconscious mind .... I know that you are there to ensure that all that is revealed will be done in a manner that is safe and beneficial for *(client's name)*.

(Remove finger from forehead).

Now *(client's name)*, we can proceed but first, for your protection, I want you now to see around you forming a white light .... a warm and comforting glow that will surround you and envelop you in its protective aura .... a safe, protective cocoon that will remain with you throughout the coming experience and beyond. Know now that I am with you at all times and that at any time .... if I touch you on the shoulder like this *(touch shoulder with a firm but gentle pressure)* .... you can then immediately safely return to this time and this place .... here .... now .... to safety and peace, and nothing can harm you or disturb you at all.

Now I am going to count to three and then snap my fingers .... and you will find yourself with me in a long corridor that stretches back through time .... right back through to the beginning of this life. You will see that there are many doors on either side of the corridor, and behind each of these doors are stored memories of this life .... some good, some bad and then some that your subconscious mind has kept from you .... as you walk along the corridor, as you pass each of these doors, you will be aware of feelings and emotions .... images .... sounds and experiences that emanate from within each of those rooms behind each of those doors. It may be that behind one of these doors is a memory that has been causing you pain in this life .... a memory of an event that needs to be addressed here and now .... your subconscious mind will guide you here and, should there be a particular door which merits your attention, you will be drawn to that door .... and you will know that, before we proceed further, that door must be opened and you must deal with what lies within that room beyond.

So go ahead now .... walk along that corridor, past each of those doors .... ahead of you at the other end of the corridor you can see in the distance a door .... so much heavier .... so much more imposing than all of those along the sides .... this is the door through which you passed into this life from beyond .... and it is this door that you must now go through to see what was before, and it awaits you now .... you have the key and it will open for you .... but you must pass by all of the other doors of this life before you can pass through this one. Go ahead now .... take your time .... if there is a door that beckons you before you reach that special door, then that is okay, and we can pause to deal with whatever needs to be done .... you can speak to me clearly now as we go ahead .... but you cannot wake .... just tell me when you are at the door to that life before .... or a door that needs to be opened here before we go on .... I am with you at all times.

(Events as they occur will determine progress. It may well be the case that the client will feel drawn to a door on this side of the veil. Here you should proceed, allowing him/her to enter that room and deal with the content which may be the cause of some problems in this life. Proceed down the corridor when the client feels able to leave that room .... into the corridor and then firmly close the door on the memory accessed, having dealt with it in an appropriate and beneficial way. You, as the therapist, must use your best judgment).

Now as you stand before that door that all those years ago you passed through to enter into this life, are you now certain that you wish to open that door and step through to whatever lies beyond?

(Await response)

Okay, that's fine, I want you now to see the key to that door in the lock .... reach out now and turn that key .... feel it turn easily .... now push open that door. Now I will count to three and on the count of three you will find yourself in a time before this time .... this life .... in a place where you have been in another time .... where you have lived before. One .... Two .... Three. .... Where are you now? Are you inside a building or outside? How old are you? .... What is your name? ....

(The questions that you ask will of necessity be in accordance with the natural progression of the client's experience. The main points at this stage are to ascertain details of age, sex, nationality and profession. Questions as to family and friends, etc. .... to determine the period in which this life was lived. I remember many years ago being advised to allow my own subconscious to help me and in this I will pass on that good advice. I personally record the sessions in order that facts which arise can be checked by the client if that is his/her wish)

(At the end of every life, there is a death, and this is a matter which can be important to the client's experience. Obviously, there can be violence, sometimes horrific events, but you have assured your client that he/she is beyond harm. Remember to use the name that is given in the life recalled when speaking to your client.)

Now (*client's name*), in a moment I am going to count from one to three and then I will snap my fingers .... you will then find yourself at that time at that place just before you pass into spirit. **"Snap"**! Please tell me where you are and what is happening to you. *(Here you will be exploring the circumstances of death - it could be sickness, violence or just old age .... the client may have died alone or with others around .... yours are the questions that will bring out the facts).*

Now, when I snap my fingers you will leave this life, passing into spirit. **"Snap!"**

Now let's go to your funeral: .... who is there? .... what does it say on your memorial?, etc. etc ....

When I snap my fingers again, I want you to find yourself in that place where all souls go between lives .... **"Snap!"** .... Describe to me now this place where you are .... are there any people in this life that you have recalled that are there with you now? Are there any people there, who will be with you in your next life, the life that you have been living before you went back to that life before?

What was the purpose of the life that you have just recalled? .... Were you successful in that life, ... achieving that purpose?

Now, as I count from one to five, I want you to find your way back to that door through which you came to this life recalled .... now go through that door into the corridor and then firmly close that door behind you and turn the key. *(Count slowly from one to five).*

Now I want you to go back to that place of comfort and safety where you were before we began the recall .... now relax and enjoy the peace and the calm tranquillity of this place .... notice now that the white light that enveloped you .... is still with you .... all around you .... that protective aura .... and as you relax deeper now .... that white light begins to enter into your body to be absorbed .... to become part of you, and you can feel its positive force .... its comforting energy as it circulates within your body now .... relaxing you .... calming you .... you feel an emotional calm that cancels out any unpleasant feelings and emotions that you may have had, and you feel more relaxed and comfortable than you have ever felt before.

In a few moments, you will be able to return to full conscious awareness. You will remember everything that is safe and beneficial for you to remember about your previous life recalled, your experience will strengthen you and help you to better understand those things in life which will remain forever unclear, and you will be aware of feelings of peace and calm .... a gentle acceptance of what is to be allows you to continue now, free of anxiety about what will be, as that new understanding deep within your subconscious is utilized to your highest benefit.

Trance termination.

(For the benefit of those like Tony Powell Dp Hp MIAH, who is unable to snap his fingers, the tapping of the desk with a suitable object will serve just as well.)

Releasing Negative Emotions

As you go deeper now .... you can be aware that negative emotions never change anything .... they are simply a waste of energy and a lost opportunity to generate beneficial emotions .... positive thoughts and feelings that will help you.

Negative emotions are hurtful .... they hurt you .... they actually damage and injure you.

When you experience .... anger .... frustration .... guilt .... or jealousy .... this is because you are not getting something that you desire. Agree with yourself right now to stop wanting things that you know you cannot have .... as you do this for yourself .... immediately you will become happier and more content with what you do have.

Agree now to change the way that you think about things .... longing for things you cannot have is ignoring and wasting the benefits and happiness that are to be enjoyed with what you do have. You now decide to enjoy and be happy with what you do have.

If you are harbouring now any negative thoughts and feelings towards others .... they only do you harm .... they actually do cause you harm and pain. Negative thoughts and negative feelings only hold you there in the past .... they prevent you from moving forward .... making progress .... making the most of your life.

If you are harbouring any negative emotions .... anger .... frustration .... or jealousy .... release these feelings .... these negative emotions now .... let them go and forever free yourself from what has been and now is no more.

If you have sadness .... perhaps for something or someone that you have lost .... grieve now for what you have lost .... or for what you never had and release that longing .... that craving .... just let it go.

If you have any guilt for something that you did .... or omitted to do .... forgive yourself .... do it now .... just let it go. You have always done your best in any situation .... you did what was right for you at the time .... or you did what you did because it was all you could do. Just release all guilt right now .... release it whole-heartedly .... just let it go.

You have always done your best .... and nobody can expect that you do more .... so accept that you are the best that you can be and let those negative feelings of inadequacy .... failure .... and guilt go.... just let them go now ....

If you have bad feelings .... feelings of betrayal .... of jealousy .... revenge .... you recognize now with clarity and understanding .... that those feelings do not benefit you in any way .... they harm you .... they hurt you and prevent you concentrating your best efforts on enjoying what you have: .... love .... and warmth .... friendship .... and so much more .... and you release those feelings .... those negative harmful emotions .... just let them go .... they have no place in your life.

When you leave here today, your subconscious will help you with new learnings and positive thoughts and emotions .... It will remind you in a very powerful manner whenever you experience a negative thought .... such as fear .... disgust .... anger .... guilt .... hatred .... jealousy .... that you have a choice .... you can control your thoughts .... control your feelings .... and decide to have only good thoughts and positive emotions .... you choose now to have only good and positive thoughts and feelings. In future you will be aware when you experience a negative thought or emotion .... and you will immediately turn it into a positive thought or emotion .... that helps you to move forward .... enjoy your life and what you do have .... love .... compassion .... understanding .... forgiveness and acceptance of what is to be.

Now you can choose to release all of those negative thoughts .... negative feelings .... right now .... immediately .... or you can choose to do this for yourself in one hour from now .... or just before you go to bed.

Now I would prefer that you release each and every negative thought and feeling right now .... but it is up to you to choose a time .... today .... which is the right time for you .... accepting that your subconscious knows what to do for you .... thinking .... without awareness .... thoughts that are beneficial and appropriate and not needing to know how it will do that for you.

Now as you go deeper .... turning inward .... becoming one with your own inner mind .... that part of you that has perfect knowledge and understanding .... I would like you to allow that part of you to do its best work for you as you present to your inner self all of those negative thoughts, feelings and emotions that have in the past hurt you .... and enjoy the warm comfortable positive feeling that embraces you now as those negatives are dealt with in a most appropriate manner .... released .... disposed of to be replaced with positive beneficial thoughts .... feelings .... and emotions.

Present to your subconscious now .... each of those negative emotions that you have experienced .... present each seven times .... and experience now the strength and the comfort as each negative emotion is transformed .... easily .... quickly .... and without effort. When you have finished this task and you are completely satisfied that all the work that needs to be done for your benefit .... has been completed .... then you can allow yourself to drift upwards .... towards the surface of awareness .... bringing with you feelings of balance .... positivity .... confidence .... and good feelings about your own self worth as a special and unique person .... allowing your eyes to open feeling refreshed .... feeling wonderful.

Sleep & Dream

The unconscious mind is interesting to observe as you drift down into that trance .... where those unconscious thoughts and images and ideas .... flash through the mind like schools of fish darting through a clear blue sea .... startling as they suddenly appear .... their strange shapes and forms .... and then disappear to be replaced by others .... beautiful .... strange .... wonderful.

Some thoughts and images are of the past .... about the present .... or about the future .... and perhaps you will know how pleasant it can seem to see that what is to come can be good .... pleasant .... and beneficial .... or perhaps that all will be sad .... unpleasant .... and detrimental .... like frightened fortune-tellers of days gone by .... predicting the end of the world .... seeing the gloom and misfortune to come in the manner in which tea leaves are left behind in a cup when all else has been enjoyed .... All they can see is what is bad.

When you look at your hands .... I wonder if what you see there is the future .... or is it the past that you see there .... or even the present? .... And is what you see there good or bad .... or just what must be there at present? .... Real fingers .... real thumbs .... and do the fingers point to the past or to what will be .... who can tell? .... And what do you make of the horoscopes in the daily papers and how they will suggest that wealth .... health .... and happiness are just around the corner .... that every cloud has a silver lining .... while the prophets of doom are abroad with their placards and slogans .... announcing the end of mankind and the wrath of heaven?

Those who are paid .... are paid attention to and have a different point of view .... but at least their messages are easy to see .... not hidden away to pop out to remind us of how bad .... how awful things could be .... telling us to beware of this, or afraid of that .... reminding us to be concerned at something that could happen .... something awful or even terrible .... and I wonder if you really do see yourself falling each time you walk down those stairs .... or trapping fingers each time that you close a door .... and how often does that terrible predicted thing occur, and how often did it **not** occur, time after time after time.

Please consider now those birds who, as soon as they are born, ...
are afraid .... They don't have to learn to fear the shape of a hawk
that soars above .... nature does that for them to protect them ....
and on some large buildings with lots of glass .... that shape of the
hawk is pasted on the glass windows to stop the birds from flying
into them and harming themselves.

The shape scares them away and that cannot be unlearned. You
know that you will not fall off the edge of the world if you sail out
to sea .... you know that tomatoes are not poisonous .... and that
toads will not give you warts .... and just believing that you can fly
.... will not make it so .... even though it can be fun to watch
Superman or Peter Pan .... like anything can be fun or not .... and
any knot can be untied .... as your unconscious mind finds its own
way to unlearn for you and see things in a different light .... a
warm .... positive .... comfortable light that allows things to change
.... feelings to change .... to rearrange those thoughts and images
.... allowing the mind to foresee that change in the future and to
enjoy noticing that change occur.

And now as you relax in that very special way .... your unconscious
mind for your benefit makes itself open to all the suggestions that I
might make here .... which are all for your benefit .... and allow
those suggestions to imprint deep in your inner mind .... firmly
fixed .... embedded so that they remain with you long after you
leave here today .... helping you to learn new ways to make those
changes that you want to make for your own sake.

And so for now .... you can enjoy that feeling of deep and special
relaxation .... aware of those inner forces empowering you ....
enabling you to grow stronger .... fitter .... more confident in your
own special abilities and capacities to do those things which are
right for you .... to concentrate your mind on those things which
are positive and rewarding.

You become aware of your special qualities .... recognize your own
true worth .... your thoughts from this moment are directed
outwards from yourself to what you sense around you .... You
become more relaxed .... steadier .... more settled .... mentally and
physically.

At the end of each day you will be pleasantly tired .... remaining calm and confident in your new-found learnings about yourself .... and you will then settle down in your bed as your unconscious mind reminds you that it really is okay to be okay and to let go now .... and to give yourself permission to sleep a deep and restful sleep .... readying you for the day to come .... a day when you will feel stronger and feel better .... and each day you will become stronger and fitter .... more alive .... more confident in your ability to look after you in a way that your subconscious will find easy .... automatic to do for you.

I will give you an anchor now .... you can know that your subconscious mind will be there to protect and guide you through the hours of the night .... letting you know that it is okay .... and to let you know that should your attention be required .... should a child call out for you .... that you are instantly awake and aware .... then you relax again and resume that restful deep slumber when all is well .... and all is well.

And now as you continue to relax .... each breath soothing you .... I wonder how much attention you have paid to the different thoughts floating through your mind .... your mind can be so active as it relaxes .... and then you can realise how difficult it is to remember what I was saying exactly seven minutes ago .... or what I was talking about nine minutes ago .... or what you were thinking about .... four minutes ago .... but doesn't it seem like too much effort to bother trying to remember? .... It takes more effort than it's worth .... and so will you remember to just relax comfortably .... when it really is too much work .... too much effort to bother at all.

And so for now you can take some time .... for yourself to go over it all and review all that you have experienced there while your body rests so comfortably here .... so go ahead now .... take a short time that can seem to be a long time .... and you can let me know when you have done all that is needed .... returning to the surface of wakeful awareness .... bringing with you that new feeling of balance and harmony .... feeling restful and relaxed .... confident and assured .... feeling absolutely wonderful .... as you appreciate what an eye-opening experience it has been.

The Final Good-Bye

For use with those clients who have lost someone and did not have the opportunity to say good-bye and to say those things that needed to be said.

Contra-indications: those who will not accept the concept of continuance of spiritual being.

(Induce hypnosis and use "The Garden" deepener)

In this beautiful and serene place where you are so comfortable and relaxed .... where peace and harmony are so natural .... you can be aware that it can be so easy to relax even deeper now as you listen to the sound of my voice .... each word a signal for you to go deeper and deeper still into profound relaxation of mind and body .... and did you know that just as you have eyes that see the world around you .... you also have an eye deep within that we call the mind's eye? .... And, just like your physical eyes, this eye has an eyelid that can close down .... as you relax, it will close down shutting out those stray thoughts and images that are not appropriate here .... and it is closing now .... closing .... closing .... and all that is there now is calm tranquillity .... feelings of peace and of capability .... of beneficial possibility.

And as you relax ever deeper you can be aware that, although you are alone in this beautiful place .... many before you have come here to enjoy and benefit from the positive healing vibrations that abound here .... and I would like you to know that you have been so very fortunate to have known that special person who has so quickly been taken from you .... fortunate that you have been able to hold such wonderful memories that have been for you so powerful .... so influential.

In this special place .... you can enjoy today a very rare and special privilege .... for here .... there in that garden of peace .... all must pass in spirit as they travel to that place beyond the gate in the wall at the bottom of the garden .... the gate that you can see now through the screen of trees .... overgrown with ivy and honeysuckle .... a gate through which you cannot pass .... yet .... for you have much to do here .... your life to live.

You can be aware of the sounds of gentle laughter .... of music and of an aura of peace that you have not yet experienced .... this is coming from beyond the gate .... in that place where all departed spirits dwell between lives .... where even now there are those who have gone before who wait for you .... watching you and lending to you the strength that they can give to you in spirit.

You are now standing before that gate .... carved and ornate, it stands firmly bolted for you are not ready to enter .... but just for a time you have the gift now of asking someone within to pass through that gate into the garden here .... and for a time you can speak with that person .... ask what you need to ask and know that the answers will be given with truth and wisdom that is no longer constrained and influenced by the matters of this world. Those beyond that gate have passed through the veil that keeps from the living the truths and the wisdom, and they now are unfettered by those earthly constraints .... All you need to do is to call the name of that person .... and they will come through that gate to speak with you. Because that person is in spirit and formless, I don't know how they will make themselves known to you .... you may see them as you know that person .... or perhaps you will experience a feeling .... an emotion that lets you know that they are there .... but you will know that that person is there .... in some safe, pleasant way and for a time you can speak with that person .... say all of those things that you want to say .... ask all that you need to ask .... and know that here there is only love.

It is different this time .... for you know that soon, very soon, he/she must return beyond the gate .... there to wait for you .... but this time you can be sure that all that needs to be said can be said and that the peace you seek can be real .... so that you can release him/her and then continue with the life that you have .... make the choices that you can make .... positive and beneficial .... moving on as you need to move on in that way which is natural and of value .... memories now kept like jewels .... pretty, and of value, which can be taken out for a time and worn .... that enhance and make splendid, as their light reflects and makes special all that is there .... and you will be there with those jewels that are yours to keep.

Please take some time now .... time to spend with that person who is here with you now .... some private and special moments .... while I wait back here for you .... to let me know when you have completed all that you can there .... resolving any remaining problems and are ready to let go .... by just saying " I have finished here".

(Wait until the client responds)

That's good .... now you need to tell that person how much you love them .... and say that last good-bye for now .... feel the love that you will carry with you .... that feeling of peace and calm inner wisdom that is yours from your experience .... go ahead now, hug that person .... and say that last good-bye .... now.

And now that person returns .... is gone now .... leaving with you that wonderful feeling of peace within .... calmness of spirit .... a sense of renewed purpose as you now drift upwards, slowly reorienting to conscious awareness, bringing with you that new feeling of balance .... harmony .... and peace .... and when you will .... your eyes will open, and you can know that what has been done here will strengthen you more each day.

Float Away Stress

As you go deeper now .... each easy breath relaxing you .... calming you .... you can be aware of how comfortable and peaceful you are becoming .... as your body relaxes and your mind relaxes with it .... all tension .... all anxiety and fear just draining away now and calm filling you completely.

* I would like you to imagine that you are in a sailing boat, all alone, floating on a lake *. all around are mountains, their steep sides covered with forests of pine trees .... their peaks snow-capped.

You have sailed to the very centre of the lake, enjoying the fresh crispness of the air and the scent of the pine forests carried on the breeze that drives the boat .... filling the sails at a gentle but exhilarating pace .... the splash and gurgle of the water as the boat cuts through the gentle swell .... the creaking of the rigging and the crack of the sails as they fill with each gentle gust of air.

You can be aware of how good you feel .... alone with your own thoughts .... alone with the sounds of nature all around .... a calm natural peace that knows no concerns or troubles .... nothing disturbs that peace .... nothing bothers you at all.

Now the wind drops to almost nothing .... the sails flap limply as they empty of the wind that drives the boat forward .... the surface of the water becomes calm .... still .... flat as a mill pond .... the surface ruffled only now and then by a gentle zephyr.

You feel the sun warming your skin .... comfortably warm .... soothing and relaxing you .... the quiet surrounds you now, broken only by the gurgle of water beneath the hull .... the faint sounds of birdsong .... the occasional splash as a fish rises to take an insect .... calm .... peaceful tranquillity surrounds you and envelops you.

You lie down on a soft cushion on the bottom of the boat, unconcerned at the lack of wind .... knowing that the engine is there and in perfect working order when and if required. You look up at the crystal clarity of the blue sky .... small clouds perfect and white hang above and around the tops of the mountains visible from where you are so relaxed and comfortable.

The still air carries the sounds of some fishermen .... casting their lines from the shore .... and there .... the distant tone of a church bell calms you .... relaxing you more with each note. High in the sky .... a jet trail marks the progress of an airliner .... etching its progress towards the far reaches of this wonderful world .... and you relax even deeper feeling within a calm, comfortable heaviness that is so pleasant .... so very nice.

The boats drifts .... rising and falling with the almost non-existent swell .... you are looking now at the very tip of the mast as it sways gently .... it appears to touch the clear blue sky above .... the air is so clean here .... you can taste it and you feel the calm tranquillity .... absorb that gentle peace .... and you drift too with thoughts that are pleasant and calming .... you breathe in peace and calm with every gentle breath .... breathing out anxiety and stress.

Here you have time to reflect on those things that have caused you stress .... you have time now to assess carefully and with a clarity never before available to you .... the importance and the relevance of so many different things. You realise that you have fallen into a habit of reacting in a manner which has proved stressful for you. You have reacted to stress in the same way that a bull responds to a red rag or to the matador's cape. You resolve now to ignore the red flags and to calmly reflect and decide on the most peaceful and effective way to live your life .... calmly .... confidently..... in control .... knowing that you are in control of you and of your life.

Things that are stressful are so because we allow them so to be .... and you are now that person who is aware that you do have the choice .... you choose to be calm and unaffected by the rush and hurry .... to make unhurried and calculated decisions that are the right ones for you and those who are important to you.

You can be aware now of the peace .... the calm .... the confidence that fills you .... expanding within you .... and you enjoy the still-ness .... the warmth of the sun .... the subtle sounds of nature all around .... the sights and the scents that can allow you to be aware of the larger world .... the depth of water beneath you..... the natural world at peace with itself .... as all troubles and cares fade into unimportance .... insignificance.

You feel so much stronger now .... aware that the strength comes from deep within you .... it was there all the time .... hidden for a time beneath turmoil and stress, but now no longer shrouded within a veil of negativity and lack of confidence, it shines through .... and you recognize the strength that is yours and resolve now to use that which is yours to your highest benefit.

As the boat drifts you know that it can be so easy *For you* to allow the prevailing winds to take you wherever they will .... but ~~in your~~ vessel you have the power when winds blow, to tack and to steer, using the winds as you choose to guide which is the right way for you .... and you have in reserve, too, that engine .... that power which can mean to you that you have complete choice in the way you go .... but it can be pleasant to drift .... knowing that you can choose freedom .... calm .... confidence and you will, will you not?

If ever you feel burdened and stressed .... you can choose to get into your boat and drift whenever you need to, whenever you want to .... using the strength that is yours, and so growing stronger and stronger with every day.

Anger & Depression

And as you relax more and more, you can know that how we feel about something imagined or real, ... is really up to us.

It's like the man I once knew who bought a car .... brand new .... his pride and joy .... and he polished it and waxed it .... vacuumed the inside at least once a week, sometimes more .... He was so proud of that car .... until one day another driver reversed into it and put a huge dent in the side .... scraped the paint work, and he was so upset and hurt that he flew into a rage at first .... he refused even to drive the car for a week .... and when he finally did drive it .... he drove it like a lunatic .... thrashing the engine and crashing the gears .... and he refused to clean it or polish it .... and every time that he saw that huge dent .... a big deep depression in the side .... he became so very angry and sad .... and sometimes he even cried.

It changed his whole life .... nothing seemed to make him happy any more .... nothing seemed like fun.

He kept looking at that dent .... which reminded him how upset he was .... how angry .... every time he saw it he felt a twinge inside .... and he thought to himself .... "Why bother? .... Why me? .... Nothing ever goes right anyway!!"

The dent began to rust .... and after a while it became an ugly hole that he glanced at every day and felt that sad .... mad feeling again.

After a while .... he just didn't want to go anywhere .... didn't want to do anything, because each time he went out .... he saw that hole again .... and felt bad again .... just as though he wanted to go inside and hide.

It was as if he wanted to feel bad .... he felt as if he had a right to .... and he was right .... but he could have done something .... because he did have insurance, unlike the people who live in areas prone to floods .... who live next to rivers or by the sea .... where everything washes away when the river overflows its banks .... or the tide comes in further than normal .... they lose everything they have .... but move back when the waters recedes .... telling others that they are just glad to be alive.

I suppose it's hard to be mad at a river or the sea .... to take a flood personally. They just call it "an act of God" and go to church to pray that it will never, ever happen again .... but they know that it most probably will .... because rivers flood and the tide rises .... just as people make mistakes or do things wrong .... It's just their nature .... the way they are, and nobody thinks that a river or the sea should be different .... or gets angry when it does what it does .... and nobody worries that they caused the rain or the high winds that caused the flood.

They just move back in and get on with their lives .... and go swimming or boating .... glad that the sun is back .... the damage undone.

Now *(client's name)*, ... whether you like it or not .... it's entirely up to you .... but if you really want to feel better .... perhaps you can pay closer attention to what you think and what you do .... because you can choose to think about things that make you feel good .... that make you sad and feel bad .... or you can begin to do things that make you feel good. .... It's entirely up to you.

You can think sad thoughts .... you can remember bad feelings, or you can replace them with a comfortable participation in things that you enjoy.

You create the space in which you live. .... You have the ability to learn how to direct your thinking in whatever way you choose.

You can change what you do .... you can do things for you. And so tonight .... tomorrow .... this week .... what I want you to do is this: .... every evening .... when you eat your evening meal .... your unconscious mind can automatically remind you .... perhaps with a particular sound .... a particular thought .... a particular image .... a stop sign of sorts .... an alarm .... that this is the time for you to decide what you will do that evening.

You can either decide to do something interesting, or something fun for a change .... or you can just decide to sit and think hard about every unpleasant thing .... about everything maddening event that has happened to you and about how upset you want to be about it.

It's completely up to you .... to enjoy yourself doing something different .... or to practise making yourself feel bad.

Self-Assertion

Direct approach for those who have lost sight of the priorities of life, and of their own abilities to make choices for themselves:

As you go deeper now, drifting to wherever your subconscious will take you, to a place where there is only peace .... calm .... and tranquillity .... and nothing concerns you other than the relaxing sound of my voice .... you can be aware that there really is no reason at all to make an effort to try to hear or to understand each and every word that I might say or not say .... Here .... as you rest quietly .... over There .... and it can be a comfort for you to know that your subconscious will hear and will understand everything that is important to you .... and it's so much easier to just allow those things to occur in their own way, while your conscious mind can drift to somewhere else entirely.

As you drift ever deeper with your own thoughts in your own way .... I would like you to pay close attention to each time I say the word .... NOW .... this will be for you a signal to go deeper still.

Many people come here to seek help with problems such as you are experiencing, and they will tell me I have no motivation .... no spark .... no zest, and my answer to them is always the same .... you have all the motivation you need, and that spark, that zest for life that once you found so readily available, is still with you, but it has become hidden .... lost within a mist of negative thoughts. But you can congratulate yourself right NOW on the fact that you found the motivation necessary to make the appointment .... and the spark of positivity to arrive here on time .... unlike that person who did not make the appointment .... did not have the motivation to make the effort .... that person is not here NOW .... sitting comfortably there .... that person was unable to distinguish the place from where they are NOW from the place where they would like to be.

You have all the motivation .... all the spark and the zest for life that you need, but there is one thing that you don't have .... yet .... and that's self-confidence .... the self confidence that it takes to set out on any journey or tackle any task, knowing that you have made all necessary arrangements and preparations .... knowing that you can .... you will .... complete that journey or that task .... easily .... quickly and without effort.

As you go deeper NOW .... please allow your subconscious to show you yourself at your place of work .... see yourself as you start your daily round of tasks .... NOW taking time to organize and prioritize those things that must be done.   See yourself calm .... confident as you begin the first of those tasks, now taking the time .... seeing that task through to completion before beginning the next on your list of priorities.

If for some unforeseeable reason the task that you have begun cannot be completed, you remain positive as you complete that task as far as you are able and then set it aside, knowing that you have done all you can and that you can proceed no further until those elements required are available to you. It now becomes a new task, and you can, without hesitation or feelings of inadequacy or guilt, continue with the next of your priorities.

Should you be disturbed from the task that you are attending to, perhaps as a colleague requires your attention to what he or she considers important and wishes to be attended to immediately, you will be aware of a deep inner calmness that comes from deep within your subconscious .... helping you to feel calm and confident as you listen attentively, and in a calm, confident manner assess for yourself the importance of the situation .... and then, as those feelings of confidence and calmness grow stronger and stronger with every moment, ... see yourself NOW asserting yourself as calm and confident .... as you make your decision .... make your conclusion as to the importance and action required.

You are NOW comfortable and calm as that person who relies on you and has confident in the knowledge which you carry within .... confident in your own ability as you exercise your calm orderly approach to everyday tasks .... as you do this .... others appreciate you more, and their confidence in you grows as you exercise these special qualities of quiet calm and confidence.

You will experience more each day the satisfaction and the self-pride that attend your new and confident manner .... and those things that in the past caused you anxiety and feelings of inadequacy are NOW easy and of no concern. You will be pleasantly surprised at how easy they become, for you NOW accept that things do not need to be difficult and hard to warrant merit.

Each new task and each new challenge is for you NOW a pleasure, because you are aware of the simple and absolute truth .... the truth that you are at your best when you are relaxed, and that the most that anyone can expect of you is that you do your best.

You can NOW be aware also that even champion athletes who strive for perfection can make mistakes and sometimes get it wrong .... and even as they do their best .... that perfection, that great ideal is so seldom required or expected. A mistake is simply an opportunity to do it better next time.

You are NOW that person that you wish the world to see .... aware NOW of your own true value as a unique and special person, looking outward from yourself to those around you, aware that you have all you need to be certain that the decisions that you make for yourself are the right decisions for you and for those who are special to you.

You NOW take the decision to be responsible and caring for yourself, for you know that in this way you can be at your best and give of your best for those whom you love and care for, and who love and care for you .... and as you do this, your true personality will shine through .... others will warm to you and the bonds will grow stronger as your relationships grow and develop. You are calm, confident .... self-assured .... your personality, once dimmed within that mist of negativity, now shines brightly as those mists dissipate .... and that spark grows bright and clear for all to see .... bright and positive.

Experience NOW that good feeling, that positive and confident feeling that is yours as you choose to make the right choice for you .... as your subconscious mind does its best work for you without the need for you to know just how it knows what to do.

You now take quality time to be with those whom you love and who love you, time that means for you that only they are important whilst you are sharing yourself .... and to them you give this time freely.

From this time forward, your subconscious will remind you, as it can, of those things that are important .... that life is for living, and that work is part of that life which can also be enjoyed .... but always that you work to live and do not live to work. You now work to enjoy the justifiable rewards of your efforts, and gone forever is that feeling that tells you that you must feel guilty whenever you find pleasure in life, with your family and friends.

You NOW accept fully and without reservation that your subconscious mind will take care of you and all that is important .... and will remind you with a calming constancy of those things that have lasting and durable value .... that are significant .... and you NOW become a friend of your own inner friend and confidant that you are NOW intensely aware of .... a wise and personal advisor deep within, with your best interests and well-being always the main consideration and motive. You NOW hear clearly and unmistakably the voice of that inner advisor .... that long lost friend and you renew that friendship, a close contact now always to be retained.

From this moment forward, you are your own person .... you NOW like, respect and love yourself more .... not in an egotistical way, but in a way that is beneficial to you as you listen to your own wise inner advisor and trust him/her to be with you at all times whenever needed.

NOW I want you to take in a deep breath, and as you expel all of the air from your lungs, go deeper NOW .... and as you turn inward to contact your own inner self, you can experience those new feelings of confidence and self esteem, that inner trust that allows you to know that you have all that you need to be the person that you wish to be as those feelings expand and grow to cocoon you NOW within a glow of warming and calming influence that allows you to always be at your best .... positive .... confident .... self-assured .... motivated and full of the spark and the zest for life that is there within.

Age Progression

A utility for allowing the new subconscious patterns to be experienced in future contexts. This can be incorporated into many sessions to provide you with a check on your work.

And now that you have had the opportunity to discover something about yourself, I wonder how many ways you'll find to use this new ability of yours creatively on your own behalf .... and it can be as if a long time has passed since this session .... a few days .... and a few months ago that we spent some time together where you learned that you could feel so good .... and you had a thought at that time that allowed you to look at yourself differently .... and as you look back over the time that has passed since then, how has that thought affected you? What things are different? What can you do now that you couldn't do then? ....

Pin-Point

Regression technique:

And now .... as you drift deeper with the sound of my voice .... into that place of safety that you can choose .... nothing bothers you or disturbs you at all .... and while we, for the purposes of this therapy, begin to explore those memories of yours .... of significance and of value .... I want you to know that I am Here with you as you rest quietly There .... nothing can harm you at all .... you can experience now a feeling of calm .... of peace .... of tranquillity.

And now I would like you to allow your subconscious to show you a railway station .... a very special railway station, where the trains that run on the track can go forward in time and also backwards to times past .... to memories of events that have occurred and have been hidden from you .... memories perhaps that are hurting you now and causing you anxiety and pain .... those memories that when exposed to the light of conscious awareness .... and your new experience and ability to form more appropriate and beneficial perceptions .... will lose their power to harm ever again.

Now experience yourself on that station .... choosing the carriage in which you will travel on that special train that will take you on that journey to past memories that are so important to you.

As you settle into your seat .... you relax deeper .... as the train begins to move off backwards into time .... as if then was now .... now is then .... as the train gathers speed .... you look out of the window .... events experienced pass by .... remembrances like telegraph poles along the track .... some instantly recalled .... some distant and vague .... so many .... so fast now .... the train gathering speed .... hurrying to where your subconscious mind knows is your important destination .... that special and important event in time .... and you can notice now that the train is slowing .... the clatter of the wheels changing note as the images that pass your window become slower and more distinct .... and now the brakes are applied .... as your subconscious mind chooses the exact moment .... the time that is now as the carriage comes to a halt and the door opens .... you step out .... and things and events are clear .... there .... now .... and you can talk to me and tell me what is happening .... who is there .... why is this important ....

The client's responses will now determine the direction and nature of the therapeutic interventions which are appropriate to use

Enuresis In Children

Have the child bring along a favourite toy such as a doll or Teddy bear that they would normally take to bed with them.

Hello *(child's name)* .... do you know why Mummy has brought you to see me today? Well, what we are going to do is play a little game that I know .... would you like that?

I see that you have brought *(Teddy or dolly)* along to see me .... would you tell me his/her name?

I bet you play with him/her a lot, don't you? .... and I bet too that you are very good at pretending, aren't you? .... Would you like to play a game of pretend with me now? Good. It's very, very easy to play .... all you have to do is just sit there as still as you can and then close your eyes for me .... can you do that? .... Mummy is going to play as well and she is going to close her eyes as well .... and I want you to pretend just as hard as you can .... that you just can't open your eyes at all .... and you can pretend so very hard that even if you want to open them .... you just can't .... and when I want you to open your eyes .... you won't be able to until I say special magic words .... When I say "Teddy says 'Open your eyes'", then you will be able to open your eyes .... but if I don't use those magic words then your eyes will shut tighter and tighter until I say "Teddy says 'Open your eyes'"...... and that's because you are pretending so well .... better than anyone else can .... that's very good.

Now as I talk to you about something very important, you can hear all of my words, but they all help you to pretend even harder than before that your eyes just will not open until I say the magic words .... and you can feel so nice and comfy sitting there in my comfortable magic chair .... nothing worries you at all .... and perhaps you can notice that you feel a little sleepy .... just a little bit .... so cosy there .... so warm .... cuddling Teddy now .... and, as I talk to you, you can think about something very important to you .... it's about that little problem that you have been having when you go to sleep in your cosy bed .... that you are so cosy and warm that you sometimes forget to remember that you need to wake up when you need to wee wee *(use the term most often used by the child)* .... you just forget to wake up and you have an accident that makes you feel so sad .... and then Mummy has to come along and change all of your bedclothes because they are all wet and uncomfortable for you .... and you really do want to remember not to forget to remember when it's so important .... don't you? .... I know that you think it would be so much better to remember not to forget .... and remember when you need to wake up and go to the toilet .... and you wouldn't even need to wake Mummy .... wouldn't it be good if you could do that every time?

Now I think that you could need just a little help from a very good friend of mine who helped me when I was a little boy, to learn how to remember to not forget to wake up in time .... and he has come here today to help you too .... he is going to show Teddy just how to help you remember every time that you need to go to wee wee .... and do you know .... he's so good at this .... you can be sure that you will never ever have that problem ever again.

My friend's name is Tommy Tinkle and he comes from a long way away .... where all of the fairies and the elves and the gnomes come from .... it's a place where all of the magic in the world comes from .... very, very special.

Tommy is five hundred and two years old .... and he even knows Santa Claus .... he helps him at Christmas to make sure that all of the children in the world get their presents on time .... he works very hard.

In a moment I'm going to call Tommy, and he has promised me that he will come here by magic to see you today .... all I have to do is say "Tommy Tinkle from over the moon, grant my wish and be here soon", and he will come right away .... but only you and I will be able to see him .... and only while our eyes are shut tight .... I am going to call him now.

"Tommy Tinkle from over the moon, grant my wish and be here soon."

My, that was quick .... he is here already, and as you are pretending so well, you can see him sitting in front of you on a little stool. He is funny looking, only as big as Teddy and just look at what he has on: .... a little red jacket with lots of silver buttons .... bright green trousers .... and yellow shoes with big buckles on the toes .... and what a funny pointed hat .... he even has a curly feather in it .... and he looks so very happy .... always laughing because he likes children very much. .... I wonder if you can count the buttons on his jacket .... how many are there? .... that's very good ....

Now (*child's name*), say hello to Tommy .... and I will tell you what he is going to do .... that he did for me when I was a little boy and found it so hard to remember to wake up in time to go to wee wee in the toilet .... a friend of my Mummy's asked Tommy Tinkle to come along and help me to remember to wake up in time .... you see, I had a teddy just like yours .... and Tommy showed my teddy just what to do and gave him some magic so that he would know just when I needed to wake up .... to go to the toilet .... to wee wee .... and I never ever had a nasty wet bed ever again .... I was so pleased and my Mummy was pleased too because she never had to get up to change those wet sheets ever again .... now he's going to do that for you .... and he is going to come over there and whisper in Teddy's ear the magic words that will help him to make sure that you always remember .... because teddies never ever forget magic words.

He will be very careful as he climbs onto the chair beside you .... so that he can whisper in Teddy's ear .... it won't take very long now .... so that Teddy will know exactly what to do for you .... Have you finished now Tommy? .... that's good .... he's nodding to me because I can't hear him like Teddy can .... perhaps you can hear him .... I know that when I was little I could hear him, but now that I'm grown up I can't .... because only children can talk to elves and hear what they say.

Now Teddy is going to show you what he has learned .... he knows exactly what to do .... and what to say to help you remember that you need to wee wee in the night .... but you must remember always to take him to bed with you .... and I know that Mummy will remember too .... Teddy is showing you now what he is going to do to wake you up .... what's he doing to you (*child's name*)? *(Wait for response, such as "He is pulling my hair" .... or "Tugging my nose" .... "Shouting in my ear")*. That's wonderful .... that is exactly what my Teddy did to me .... Now Tommy has to go because he is very, very busy .... so say "thank you" to him and "good-bye" now. "Good-bye Tommy, good-bye."

Now Teddy knows what to do .... and what to say .... he has all of the magic to help you never, ever forget .... now you can take him home .... and you will always remember to take him to bed with you every night, then he will be there to wake you when you need to wee wee, and you will never, ever have a nasty wet bed ever again .... so you will remember .... won't you?

You have been so very good at pretending and playing this little game with me, that Tommy has asked me to tell you that he is going to speak to Santa Claus and tell him just how good you have been .... and he is going to tell the tooth fairy to leave you something very special when she comes to see you.

Now I am going to say those magic words so that you can open your eyes and be very happy and proud at being so clever at pretending here with me today.   "Teddy says 'Open your eyes'."

Flyaway

Script for fear of flying.

And now as you relax and go deeper .... I would like you to imagine that you are at an airport .... that you are here at the airport because you are going on the holiday of a lifetime to .... (*insert chosen destination*). You have packed all you need for the journey and for your holiday .... visas are all in order .... passports are safe and you have the tickets for your journey safe and secure.

I want you to notice that you are feeling calm and confident .... you are relaxed, and have only a small and understandable anticipation and concern .... appropriate feelings towards the coming adventure.

All around you are people arriving and departing .... to and from all the exotic and not so exotic parts of this world .... You hear strange languages .... see colourful and interesting national costumes as the people hurry to and fro.

The atmosphere is of calm and practised efficiency .... people moving through the terminal .... all possible problems have a solution .... everyone and everything is taken care of, and all arrive and depart efficiently and calmly .... so much order .... so many potential problems anticipated .... the solutions readily to hand.

You now move to the desk where you will check in your luggage .... and you are aware of the procedures to ensure that all baggage is checked and weighed ....x -rayed before being allowed to be stowed away in the aircraft that will deliver you to your destination.

And all the while .... the captain and his crew are checking the aircraft systems as they do before any flight .... they check every small thing in a specific and detailed manner .... in accordance with the check-lists that are standard to the aircraft .... check lists that have been developed through many thousands of hours of experience of the technology which is ever evolving through the years.

The captain will check that everything is as it should be, because he is aware that things can go wrong .... he has natural and professional caution and has learned that the systems that he depends upon are the best that can be relied on .... he checks because he is aware that thousands of aircraft fly millions of miles each day without mishap, as all of the captains check each and every flight, because they, too, want to be as sure as they possibly can that everything is okay .... he has confidence in the engineers who service the aircraft in accordance with strict schedules and limits .... confidence in the technology that he has to support him .... so much confidence because he spends so much of his life flying others from place to place across the globe .... but he reserves for himself that natural and appropriate respect for those things that can be checked and, when he has checked them, the confidence to know that he has done his work well .... left nothing to chance, and that he will arrive safely and without fuss, just one amongst many who fly the world almost without being noticed at all by those of us who travel only now and then .... every mile is logged and every second recorded as the journey continues .... a vast and international network .... working to international rules that all must comply with and adhere to .... and thereby safety is assured .... and the captain too must be checked .... he must pass inspection and he is subject to regular and stringent health checks every six months.... performance checks .... carefully monitored to ensure that he is fit to fly .... and I wonder if you are aware that when flying, both he and his co-pilot by regulation must be served different meals, to ensure that if the food is tainted, ... there will always be a qualified and capable pilot in charge of the aircraft.

Every system on the aircraft has a back-up system .... sometimes even three or more .... and you will be pleasantly surprised at how calm and confident you will be as you board the plane .... as you are shown to your seat .... aware of the quiet efficiency of the cabin crew as they ensure that you are comfortable .... just one more flight for them in their busy schedule .... and their air of calm and confidence will allow you to become more and more calm and more confident .... feeling safe and secure.

But you will experience .... and you will be aware of a natural and appropriate anticipation .... the anticipation that you feel whenever you undertake a new and exciting adventure .... enjoying the thrill .... enjoying the thrill of the anticipation of that new experience ....

and you will be aware of a voice from deep within your subconscious .... a voice telling you that all is well and it really is all right to feel okay .... the voice of your own inner advisor .... that part of you that has perfect knowledge, and you can feel safe and secure in the knowledge that your inner advisor has all the knowledge that it needs to feel satisfied with the situation and will allow you to feel at ease .... safe .... excited .... and secure .... to see things in a different light, a warm and comfortable light that allows a feeling to change .... to rearrange those thoughts and images .... allowing the mind to foresee that change in the future .... and to enjoy noticing as that future change occurs.

You will enjoy your flight and look forward with pleasure to a new experience .... always aware of the fact that you have perfect knowledge and your own wise inner advisor to remind you to exercise normal and natural appropriate caution in all things.

Fast Allergy Cure

Step 1   *Ask client to explain how he/she feels when having an allergy attack. Get him/her to describe all symptoms.* What happens to you? Where are you? What do you hear, see and feel?

Step 2   *Instruct the client to close his/her eyes. Then:* I want you now to think about when you are having an attack, to experience all of those uncomfortable sensations as you are having that attack. *(Reiterate the symptoms and discomforts obtained from step one).* Now pump up all of those feelings and symptoms. Make them as strong as you can. *Anchor, by touching the back of the client's hand.* .... Now let those feelings pass.

Step 3: *Ask the client to open his/her eyes and explore the feelings and sensations.*

Step 4: *Ask the client to think of something pleasant. Then ask him/her to describe the sensations and feelings when he/she is not suffering an allergy attack, when things are normal.*

Step 5: *Describe the operation of the immune system. Describe the presence of marker cells whose job it is to identify harmful objects such as germs and viruses that have entered our body, and killer cells whose job it is to latch on to and destroy foreign organisms. When someone develops an allergy, the immune system is mistakenly triggered into action by a benign substance which it then marks and attacks, causing an allergic reaction.*

Step 6: *Ask the client to again close his/her eyes. Then continue:* Now imagine that it is the sort of day when conditions are such that you will suffer an allergy attack. Now as you sit so comfortable and relaxed over there, I would like you to see right across the room in front of you. There is a solid, unbreakable glass screen, about four inches thick, and on the other side of that screen I want you to see *(client's name)* walking along with his/her immune system operating efficiently, the micropansies doing their work efficiently, marking the foreign bodies and the killer cells destroying them appropriately.

Touch back of hand (Anchor) .... Now notice how good you feel, and how well and appropriately your immune system is working for you. And now *(client's name)*, I want you to just float back into the room, here to where you are sitting. There, allow those good feelings and appropriate actions on the part of your immune system to integrate now, let those efficient and appropriate immune system reactions strengthen and integrate fully and completely.

Step 7: *Now allow anchors to subside and carry out a test.:* If you were in that situation where you used to suffer from that allergic reaction; *(Describe situation, allow client time.)* tell me how you would be feeling now.

If you have been successful, the client will describe, feeling well and without the symptoms previously experienced.

Anxiety / Worry

Now that you are so very relaxed, your mind is receptive and open to new ideas .... ideas that will help you to stop worrying and enjoy life much much more.

Worrying is in fact looking into the future, predicting what might be, but focusing on only that which could go wrong.

When we care very much about someone .... or something .... it is no surprise when we worry; .... it's not pleasant, but it is natural and it is understandable. However, if there is no crisis, or when a crisis is over, we should stop worrying, relax, and enjoy life.

Because everyone needs to relax at times, even champion athletes who are under a great deal of pressure to perform, and sometimes need to be perfect to win, even they need some way to relax and to put things into perspective, to recognize that it is just a sport and not a war between nations. Because a war is one thing, and a game is something else entirely, especially in this nuclear age where a war could mean the end of everything. We really cannot afford to make the smallest of mistakes, and so some people are terrified that the fail-safe system will fail, and that will be the end of it, all because of some small error .... someone doing something wrong or saying something wrong at the wrong time, or to the wrong person, in the wrong way. Then everything goes up in flames.

Which is why they have special programmes for the people who are working with these systems, because what they have to do is so dangerous and terribly important that special training and counselling is required. This is probably the only place and situation in the world perhaps where mistakes cannot be allowed, and it is comforting to note that in almost every other place and situation, an error is just an opportunity to do it differently later on, because perfection is seldom needed and rarely required, and even champion athletes are never perfect all the time, and sometimes get it wrong. It is like the Navaho Indians who, when they weave their beautiful rugs and blankets, always leave a knot, an imperfection, so that the gods will not be angered and think that the weaver is trying to be a god.

But that is another story about what is really important and what is not, and how it feels to give yourself permission to enjoy the feeling of freedom to feel safe doing those things, knowing that the world will not end if you leave a knot somewhere, so that the gods will know that you are not challenging them, just doing the best that you can, and letting it go at that.

To overcome your tendency to worry, follow this simple two step formula:

1. First promise yourself that you will not worry about the small things.
2. Realise now that it's all small things.

We both know that you have an active mind and a reactive body, and if you think that scary thought for just one brief moment, then it has been scaring you. We also know that there are other things that you can think which are comfortable and calming, relaxing and reassuring thoughts or images that you can use instead, to help you to relax, to retain that relaxed, calm feeling.

You can let your unconscious mind learn all it needs to know to be able to distract you from those scary thoughts, to be able to provide you with those relaxing thoughts and images.

And I think that you will enjoy being happily unconcerned, unable to remember to worry in exactly the same way or at the same time. So from now on, when you enter that situation, you can enter it knowing that you are protected and can tell that part of you that tries to do its job by telling you that there are things to be afraid of here, that you really don't need it anymore. So it can either go away or find a different game to play, and remind you instead of all the good things that might happen here, or of all the fun things that might occur later, because those old thoughts and fears just aren't useful anymore.

So you can relax and forget it, go on about your business, surprised to discover perhaps that you have been thinking about something else entirely. And you will know at that point, deep down in every cell of your being, that you won't ever have to feel that way again, that it is over and done with, more rapidly than you expected. You can do it now and you can do it later, you can frighten yourself with that thought, or you can calmly relax yourself with a different thought. That's right, ... so practise and choose, it all belongs to you.

That Quiet Inner Voice

For use with clients who need to become aware of their own capabilities and gain confidence in their own inner awareness and capacities for self determination.

As you continue .... drifting .... deeper with each breath that you take .... you can be aware of how little you need to be aware of .... the sounds in the room .... the ticking of the clock perhaps .... the rustle of papers .... sounds outside .... Each sound helps you to relax even more deeply .... each word that I utter is just a signal for you to become less and less aware of the importance of all that is unimportant here .... the exact meaning of words that are said or not said as I talk to you here .... nothing bothers or concerns you as your conscious mind drifts off to a place which is comfortable and safe .... and your unconscious mind takes on the responsibility for guiding and directing your awareness .... down .... into your innermost self .... aware now of that gentle connection .... communication with that part of you that is the essence of you .... that knows all .... remembers each and every event that has served to shape and mould your unique and special personality .... a part of you that you really do hear as a quiet and calm voice from within .... a voice of wisdom and of truth that is so often lost within the clamour and the clatter of the world .... the demands .... the constraints .... the noise that is those who would have you bend to their will .... now hear that voice still, quiet and calm .... but now clear as crystal .... piercing through the fog of indecision and lack of confidence .... unmoved and unaltered in its determination to give to you at all times .... good council .... wise answers and solutions to all problems .... to your highest benefit and of those who are special to you.

This is that creative and special part of you .... that wise inner advisor that is always there for you with your benefit and well-being always the prime consideration .... a constant, etheric part that is you and was you before there was awareness of this existence in this time .... an invaluable friend that must be listened to .... and you will, will you not?

Roger P. Allen

You can recognize now that value, that unique capacity and capability that is yours .... has always been yours .... and I really don't want you to know too much how good you can feel with that intense awareness of confidence in your ability to make changes and decisions in your life for yourself .... no longer allowing others to manipulate you .... to take advantage of you .... you expect of yourself everything that is yours .... that you deserve .... that you are entitled to as a unique and special person .... aware of who you are .... aware of your own talents and special qualities .... always that person who is the forefront .... always there with a valuable input to every situation .... you listen and take note of what is important, and then you make a decision .... you make your own decision, and are comfortable in that.

I wonder if you can notice soon how others will come to rely on you to be the person that you are .... confident and self-assured .... an example to those who will admire you as you allow those qualities so long hidden .... to burst forth from within .... to astound and confound those who would manipulate and control .... you are your own person .... proud .... confident .... taking responsibility for your own life and well-being .... a true friend of your own wise inner advisor .... that is you personified.

Confidence-Building

Firstly (*client's name*), ... I would like to extend my congratulations on your decision to seek help and to allow yourself the experience of coming here today. I appreciate that you made the effort to make an appointment and to arrive on time.

Already now .... you know that you can do that ... it is in fact easy to do .... and what about that feeling of achievement .... how it feels to realise that what was easy first time, will be even easier in the future .... for it is from positive experience that you learn how to use your confidence in a way that builds and grows stronger every day .... increased self-worth .... recognising even more than before that only good and positive thoughts are of value to you .... negative thoughts harm you .... you allow only good and positive thoughts.

It's so very easy to be that person who does not allow for mistakes to be made, and it can be a comfort to know that an error is simply an opportunity to do it differently next time.

Perfection is almost never needed, and even those champion athletes are never perfect all of the time .... and sometimes get it wrong. .... It's interesting to observe that when the Navaho Indians weave their beautiful rugs and blankets, they always leave a knot .... an imperfection .... so that the gods are never angered and think that they are trying to be gods themselves.

It can be comforting to know that you can give yourself permission to feel safe and enjoy those things that are important, knowing that the world will not come to an end if you leave a knot .... so that the gods know that you are not challenging them. Just doing the best that you can and leaving it at that.

As you go deeper now, just listening to the sound of my voice .... you can be aware of those comfortable heavy feelings of legs, of arms, of the entire body that seems to float in time and space .... those hypnotic sensations that allow you to know that you have travelled from one state of awareness into another state in a calm and confident way. And I wonder now if you can allow those

99

feelings to continue .... those comfortable, relaxed sensations of mind and body .... as you drift and dream .... and my voice drifts with you.

You now look to the future in the way that tells you that things will go well .... that you will succeed .... that you are special .... attractive .... intelligent and capable .... In this way, you program yourself to succeed and you will succeed. You now look to the future and see only good things and good people happening to you as you move forward to grasp opportunities .... seeing those opportunities, clearly .... intensely aware that all of your worthwhile goals are attainable.

You have all the confidence you need to build upon, all the capabilities and capacities to be that person that you want to be, special and exciting. You and you alone have your best interests at heart, you now take control of your life. Now .... you are taking control .... you trust your own judgement in all things and you know that you alone have your best interests, and the best interests of those who are close to you, within your control .... and it is with profound satisfaction now that you undertake and commit yourself to your own best interests, utilising to your highest potential, YOUR capability, YOUR special qualities, accepting YOUR feelings of self congratulation as you achieve your worthwhile goals.

You find it easy to concentrate on what is important to you .... your subconscious mind helps you in those ways, reminding you of your successes, of your positive abilities, of all your special qualities. Others appreciate you more as you demonstrate your confidence. Your positive approach allows those around you to have confidence in you, as your confidence grows and manifests itself in your day-to-day success. Now your creativity discovers new ways of releasing itself, to become effective and part of your own special personality. You impress and amaze all with your clarity of thought and expression of new ideas and input to every situation. Once the bystander .... now at the forefront, establishing yourself as that interesting positive person that you are. You can now .... be aware that you are the equal of all, relaxed and comfortable in every situation. You are realising, now with greater clarity each and every day, that you can unlearn that feeling of fear and lack of confidence. You now take a deep breath, relax yourself from head to toe, and take the image into your mind of you .... happy and secure .... confident and self-assured, as you tell yourself .... I CAN .... I WILL. This comfortable, pleasant image soothes your mind, and all fear and self-doubt leave you completely.

You unlearn fear by being positive and realising that the only thing that can hurt you, is the fear itself. No longer do you accept fear or negativity, you banish in their entirety all unwanted, inappropriate thoughts and symptoms, allowing only good thoughts and positive feelings to grow and become part of your special personality. You do this easily because you are in control. It will become easier and easier for you to do this as you take control, and you will take control, will you not? *(Await response.)*

As you go deeper now, in control, just listening to the sound of my voice, your subconscious mind shows you yourself at that time .... that place .... when you really felt confident, ... a time when you really felt good ..... when you were the centre of attention, loved and admired. Being congratulated by those around you as you received an award for achievement .... or realised a long-standing ambition. It doesn't matter where it was or when it was, just as long as you felt really good about yourself and about your achieve-ment. Think of your finest hour, and get that image into your mind as you were at that time, at that place. You see yourself right now as the centre of attention, with all others cheering you .... congrat-ulating you .... Now hold that feeling .... Allow that feeling to be something that you can expand. Now see that special feeling as a pulsating white light, warm and comfortable .... powerful .... allow that white light to expand and grow so that it encompasses you, so that you are completely contained within a brilliant cocoon of pulsating white light. Feel that warm and comfortable feeling .... confident and admiring thoughts about you and your special quali-ties and capacities. Feel it growing .... expanding, filling your very being with its power and positive influence. And now allow that white light to be absorbed into your body, as you absorb completely and permanently, to your highest benefit, all those good and capable qualities which ensure that from this moment forward, you are the confident and self-assured person that you want to be, that you are right now.

Each and everything thing you do, you do better than you have ever done before. You approach each new task with complete ease of mind knowing that you are relaxed and in a perfect frame of mind, ... calm .... relaxed and confident. Every day your confidence grows; .... that means that tomorrow your confidence grows and the day after it grows stronger than before. As you practise being more and more confident, so your confidence grows and becomes stronger as more and more .... your feelings of self-worth become strong and powerful. Each day, with each new situation .... whenever you need to, you take control, calm your mind, disregard troubles and you are calm .... relaxed .... poised .... competent .... and confident .... You are your own person .... is that not so?

(Wait for response and then go to trance termination)

Confidence Booster

As you become more and more relaxed and less tense each day .... so .... you will remain more relaxed .... and less tense when you are in the presence of other people .... no matter whether they be many or few .... no matter whether they be friends or strangers.

You will be able to meet them on equal terms .... and you will feel much more at ease in their company .... without the slightest feeling of insecurity or inferiority .... without becoming self-conscious or embarrassed in any way.

You will become so deeply interested .... so deeply absorbed in what you are saying .... that you will concentrate entirely upon this to the complete exclusion of all else.

Because of this you will remain perfectly relaxed .... perfectly calm and self-confident .... and you will become less conscious of yourself and your own feelings.

You will consequently be able to talk quite freely and naturally .... without being worried in the slightest by the presence of any other persons. If you should begin to think about yourself .... you will immediately shift your attention back to your conversation .... and you will no longer experience the slightest nervousness .... discomfort or uneasiness.

The moment that you get up to speak .... all of your nervousness will disappear completely .... and you will feel completely relaxed .... completely at ease .... and completely confident. You will become so deeply interested in what you have to say .... that the presence of an audience will no longer bother you in the slightest .... and you will no longer feel confused .... uncertain .... or conspicuous in any way.

Your mind will become so fully occupied with what you say .... that it will make you feel confident about what you are saying. Nervousness, feeling self-conscious or embarrassed will be but a memory of past behaviour .... because you will remain throughout .... perfectly calm .... perfectly confident and totally self-assured.

Self-Esteem Booster

Imagine that you are wearing a sign that tells the world "I am a unique and very special person". You always wear that sign .... that badge and you wear it with pride. Every day you become more and more aware of your assets and the qualities and beauty within you.

You now place your complete trust in you .... in your own inner mind .... the values and opinions that you accept are your own .... you make up your own mind .... you trust your own judgment .... opinions and values .... relevant .... informed and special.

Decisions that you have been putting off will be easier now because you trust you and your ability to make those decisions which are the right ones for you and those you love .... those who are special to you and rely on you and your special wisdom .... strength .... all those qualities and capacities are within you.

You admire yourself .... like yourself, and trust yourself so much more .... others too find it easy to like you .... to respect you .... to admire you .... to love you .... but you no longer worry or concern yourself about what others think of you .... it matters only that you like and respect yourself.

You are aware that you cannot please everybody and that the only way to be successful in what you do is to trust your own judgment and to please yourself .... what is right for you will be right for those who are close to you. As you do what is right for you .... always trusting your own judgment .... having that belief in yourself .... you now have the confidence to do what you want to do .... Those who would manipulate you and take advantage of your easy-going nature ..... are now confounded .... aware that with due consideration .... you do what is right for you and those who are important to you.

You trust your own judgment and meet your own special and legitimate needs and the needs of those who are close to you and who are special. You meet those needs .... you are independent and self-sufficient.

Changes are happening within you .... changes for the better .... some you will be aware of now .... others you will be unaware of until some time in the future.

As you trust yourself more and more .... your subconscious mind will cause these ideas to be made available to you .... ideas for your benefit.

These ideas will be absorbed for your betterment so that you can easily overcome any problem. Know and believe .... whatever the mind can conceive .... the mind can achieve. Whatever you believe you can achieve .... you will achieve. Every day you are feeling more and more comfortable within yourself and you are becoming your own best friend. Every day you love and respect yourself more, not in an egotistical way .... but in a way that is positive .... natural and constructive .... and can be only beneficial to you.

Take a moment now to enjoy the feeling of liking yourself and being happy and content with the unique and special person that you are.

Know and believe that each and every small part of your mind .... your body and your spirit is an important .... wonderful and beautiful part of nature. Spirit means your higher self .... that part of you which is inspired .... strong .... kind .... loving and happy .... all of those good and special qualities that are to be admired. Those special qualities are an integral part of your unique person- ality and are there for you whenever you need them. If there are things that you have done in the past that you regret .... now is a good time to forgive yourself. Forgive yourself now and release yourself now from the shackles of those negative elements which prevent you from moving forward. Now you can be that person that you want to be.

If there are any things which others have done to you in the past .... now is the time to forgive those others. Forgive others now and release yourself right now from the past .... you now live for the moment .... this moment. Now you are that person that you want to be .... a true friend of your own personal and wise inner advisor who is you personified.

The Filing Cabinet

For use in analysis to assist the client to access relevant memories, re-evaluate and dispose of uncomfortable repressions.

Now as you relax more and more .... each word that I utter is just a signal for you to go deeper now. We are going to be working directly with your subconscious mind.

You will recall that I have told you that every memory .... dream .... event in your life is stored in your unconscious mind .... good .... bad .... insignificant .... it's all there stored .... rather like a filing cabinet .... and now your subconscious will assist you here to go through that filing cabinet, seeking memories of importance to you .... of significance that relate to your problems .... memories .... feelings and emotions that will be beneficial for you to recall here in the course of your therapy.

Just relax .... deeper now .... and allow yourself to drift along one passage of your mind until you can see a faint outline .... of a grey door. As I count to three, with each count see it becoming clearer. 1 .... becoming clear now .... 2 .... clearer still .... 3 .... you can see it really clearly now .... as you draw nearer and nearer to that door. Closer and closer now .... reach out now and open the door .... now enter into the room beyond that door .... and close the door behind you.

You can see now that you are in a cream painted room .... well-lit and airy .... even though you cannot see the source of the light, you will see everything. In the centre of the room is a plain, wooden table .... to the side of the table is a tall filing cabinet with four grey drawers .... and one black drawer at the bottom. There is nothing else at all in the room. As you walk over to the cabinet .... notice the label attached to the black drawer .... the red print says clearly .... not to be opened .... not to be read.

The grey drawers contains all of those day-to-day memories of your life .... mostly happy .... some sad .... everything that you have seen .... done .... heard .... or experienced; .... memories that are available to you at all times to help you with each new experience.

The black drawer however .... contains memories that your subconscious has decided to keep from you .... to hide from you .... and the answer to the problems that you have are there in that drawer .... that memory or memories that form for you the basis of so much hurt and pain .... so much misery. Within this drawer are those memories that, once shown to the light of conscious aware-ness, cannot be re-filed in a hurtful way .... or cause you problems ever again. Hidden away .... yes .... they caused you problems and pain .... but once brought out into that light of awareness they lose that power to cause you problems ever again, just as if they were never there.

You have come here to understand .... and to resolve your problems. By using this opportunity to examine those hidden files .... you can resolve them .... easily .... quickly .... and permanently. You cannot see your subconscious mind .... since it is formless .... but as you wait now by the table .... the black drawer will begin to slide open .... silently .... on well-oiled runners. As it slides open .... you can see the label on the drawer being removed as if by invisible hands .... torn in half .... and then dropped onto the floor.

You are now free to examine everything in the drawer. Look inside and you will observe a number of ordinary brown files. From here .... I can't see how many files there are in the drawer, but you .... there .... can see and you can count them now. Tell me *(client's name)*, how many files are there?

Inside each of these files is a piece of paper, or perhaps several sheets. Each sheet will have on it a word or words written or printed upon it, ... perhaps in black ink .... perhaps in coloured ink. You may find that some of the sheets have no writing at all, but a picture .... a drawing or a photograph which you will recog-nize and find easy to understand.

Now your subconscious is taking out the first file .... laying it open on the table .... handing to you the first page .... it is in your hands now. Look at it .... and tell me what you see.

There may be only one word on the page or it may be covered with writing or with pictures .... look at the page .... let what happens happen: .... you are looking at memories and they cannot harm you.

As you reach the end of the page, turn it over and examine the back .... there may be further detail.

What is on that page? It is no longer a secret .... dark and hidden .... no longer the unknown .... its power to harm you has gone .... it no longer has that power. Now that piece of paper is of no further use. Lay it quietly on the table for your subconscious to dispose of safely .... in any way it sees fit. Then go and take out the next file.

(Continue until the client tells you that the drawer is empty).

Now that you have had this opportunity .... and you have seen all that was hidden away from you for such a long time .... you have been able to see and to understand what has been causing your pain. Now that you know what was there, it can no longer hurt you in that way and cause you problems ever again.

Now watch, as the drawer begins to change colour .... that deepest black now fading to become grey .... the same as the others .... now ready to store new and pleasant memories for the future.

Snapshots

This is a strategy to move client into accessing memories that are important during analysis.

Now in this relaxed and comfortable situation, your subconscious for your benefit will accept my suggestions which are for your benefit and welfare in the context of this therapy .... here as you listen to the sound of my voice and the words that I say or do not say here..... and each word relaxes you as you go deeper into relaxation with each word that I utter.

I would like you now to allow your subconscious to show you a room .... a well-lit room that is very warm and comfortable .... a room where you feel totally safe and secure .... in the centre of the room is a large table that is there for you .... and there is a comfortable chair there just for you .... now walk across to that chair and sit down and become ten times more deeply relaxed.

As you go deeper now, you can see that on the table, there is a large wooden document box, a very old box, and you will see that on the table, beside the box, there is a key to that box .... Now you can pick up that key and find that it fits the lock on that box perfectly, and it turns easily as you unlock that box.

Now look inside the box and find it full of mementos of your life .... there are albums filled with photographs of all manner of things .... objects, things that you will recognise, ... most of them unimportant .... but some of great importance to you, of significance and of value here. These are snapshots of your life, hidden for so long in the deepest parts of your subconscious memory; yes, they may have cause you pain and problems in the past, but now, exposed to the light of day and to your conscious mind, they lose their power to cause you pain.

It is for you now to take out those albums from that box. I cannot see how many there are, but I know that you are able to see clearly now, and find that special album of significant importance and value to you now, just one in particular that stands out now in some way that your subconscious will understand indicates that here within are the answers to your problem(s).

Find that album now and place it on the table in front of you. Now you can begin to examine the contents of that album, so open it up at the first page and then examine it carefully and tell me what you see that is of importance to you, of significance and of value. You can speak to me clearly but you cannot wake .... Now go ahead, aware that I am here to help you and that you are perfectly safe and secure. All within that album are but memories, they do not have any power to harm you in any way. Now tell me *(client's name)* .... what do you see here? .... what do you feel? .... what are you experiencing?

Continue to deal with each page and it contents in turn, and then, in a significant manner, have the client dispose of the material - tear it up, or throw it into the fire, or whatever seems appropriate. Ensure that any photographic negatives are also destroyed at the same time, and assure the client that he/she can be satisfied that no other copies exist.

The Three Doors

Strategy for eliciting repressed memories.

And now as you relax and go deeper .... please allow your subconscious to show you yourself Here standing There in a corridor .... You feel totally safe and secure .... the corridor is well-lit, although you cannot determine the source of the light. The floor is carpeted with a thick pile carpet, and you can be aware that the colour of this carpet is a colour that your subconscious knows to be relaxing. Tell me *(client's name)*, what colour is the carpet there?

You see that this corridor has three doors and that each of these three doors has a number on it .... 1 .... 2..... or 3.

Behind each of these doors are kept all of your life memories .... not one single experience has been missed .... all are stored there .... here .... safely stored. Doors 1 & 2 are painted grey .... behind these doors are all of the ordinary memories of your life .... some happy, some sad .... all of the everyday ups and downs of life .... thoughts, images .... all of the emotions attached to each of those memories are there .... there for you to recall as experience .... wisdom ....likes and dislikes .... ways of doing things and ways of coping with each new experience that life offers you. Door 3 is different .... this door is painted the deepest black .... a door that has been for such a long, long time kept securely locked .... the key hidden from you by your own subconscious.

Hidden from your awareness are memories that are uncomfortable .... tragic .... black, guilty secrets .... memories of hurt and sadness .... of anger and frustration .... evil memories that, whilst hidden and secret, form the basis for so much hurt and misery for you. Behind that door lie the answers to problems that now affect the quality of your life .... memories whose power lies in the fact of their secrecy .... memories that will lose their power when that door is opened and they are exposed to the light of conscious awareness .... lose their power to hurt you and cause you problems ever again .... You will be free.

Your subconscious mind will now show you the key .... see it now floating in front of you .... and as you watch, that key moves to the lock and now in the lock .... it turns easily and silently, and that door slowly opens wide.

You are here .... in that corridor there to resolve your problems .... to understand .... and now you can enter into that room and resolve them easily and permanently. As you enter the room, you notice that the door remains open wide .... within this room is your unconscious .... you cannot see it because it is formless, but as you wait there for just a moment, it will reveal itself to you in some safe way that you will understand .... and it will reveal to you in some manner .... it may be visual .... a face perhaps or a familiar place .... or perhaps a sound .... a voice or even music .... it may allow you to experience its presence by way of a feeling .... but you will understand as it begins now to reveal to you the very source of your problems.

It may show you pictures .... or words .... a drawing perhaps .... maybe in colour, or in black and white .... a photograph perhaps .... whatever it is, you will know it and understand it. Whatever your subconscious mind shows you here .... is okay and safe for you to look at .... You are looking at memories .... so now look around the room and whatever happens .... just let it happen .... Whatever you are shown is right for you now to know about .... perhaps a secret exposed .... and because it is exposed .... its power to hurt you will be gone .... over, once and for all time.

Tell me what you see .... what you are experiencing as you enter into that room now.

I explain to the client that once they have dealt with all of the memories important to them in the room, the power of those memories to harm them will be negated. Once they are satisfied that they have done all that is necessary, I tell them to go out into the corridor and then to close the door. If they have done all that is required, then the door will close easily, but if there are still matters that need to be dealt with, then the door will not close. Tell them to go ahead, "Can you close the door?" I f the answer is "No", then they have not finished, and they must go back to confront whatever is preventing them from moving on.

As your subconscious mind has revealed these secrets to you for your understanding .... I wonder now if you have noticed that the door is now beginning to change colour.... changing now to grey just like the other two .... the room is empty now and ready to store new memories .... positive and pleasant memories for the future.

Smoking Therapy

*As a practising hypnotherapist, you can expect that a good propor-
tion of those who come to you for help will be smokers seeking to
quit their habit. Hypnotherapy has the reputation of being the best
therapeutic help for smoking cessation available, with an excellent
success rate.*

*When asked what the rate of success is, I always tell my clients that
I am not able to be exactly accurate, as those who come to see me
and who stop smoking will invariably forget to tell me in six months
whether they are continuing not to smoke. The only really reliable
indication I have is when a client is referred to me by another, and I
have an encouraging number of those.*

*I have heard some therapists claim a 60% or 70% success rate, and
some even higher, but how they are able to come up with these
figures without indulging in a lengthy survey over several years, I
am not really sure. I am sure that if I have two clients and both are
successful, then I can quote, quite tongue-in-cheek, a success rate of
100%!*

*I find that it pays to be honest and sometimes quite blunt with
people who call. It takes some nerve to tell someone who is going to
pay you for the service you provide that, unless they really want to
stop smoking, they may as well not bother wasting your time and
their money.* "If you really do want to stop smoking, then fine, I will
make an appointment for you right now to come along, but I have
to say this to you: if you are not sure whether you want to stop or
not, but perhaps just thinking that you will come along and see if I
can stop you, then please don't bother me and waste your money."
*Make plain to your prospective clients that you need their full co-
operation if you are to be able to help them to help themselves in that
way.*

"How many sessions will I need?" *This can be the subject of some
debate within the profession. There are differing views, but myself I
work on a simple premise: provided that the client's smoking habit is
not evidently part of the symptomology of some deeper and more
complex problem, and can be safely defined primarily as habitual,
then the problem can be resolved in just one session. If it doesn't*

work the first time, then it is not going to work. There are other factors at work here, and they need to be resolved before this coping mechanism can be dispensed with.

During the initial interview and fact-finding exercise, you, the therapist, will be able to determine from the demeanour of your client whether or not you will have to deal with other factors before you can help your client to give up the symptom that is his/her smoking. This comes with experience, and that I cannot give you here.

My 'Stop Smoking' session begins with a discussion about the client's life-style, his/her family and relationships. I want to know about the stresses in his/her life; what is important; what frightens him/her; his/her aspirations and motivations: in essence, what are the controlling influences in their life.

I want to know how they started and when; what they remember about the first cigarette smoked; why they chose to continue when the first cigarette was so awful. The answers to these questions are usually pretty much the same. "Mum and Dad smoked, and it seemed to me that I could count myself grown up when I too began to smoke." "My friends all smoked, and it seemed to be the thing to do to be one of the crowd." *(Peer pressure).* "I started in order to annoy my parents and show them they couldn't tell me what to do". *Whatever the answers, they will invariably point to the association with being grown up, one of the crowd, more sophisticated and mature, establishing independence.*

What do you get from cigarettes? *Once again the answers are so predictable.* "It helps me to relax." "It helps me to concentrate." "It calms me down." "It's something to do with my hands." "It gives me an excuse to have a break."

I have yet to hear a declaration, "It make me smell nice and attracts people to me.", *or* "I will live longer and stay healthy longer." *or* "I really do need to get rid of this money that I would otherwise spend on luxuries and things that really matter."

I ask when they smoke, beginning with when they wake in the morning. Before breakfast, after breakfast, in the car, on the telephone, after a meal, with a cup of tea, and so on.

I ask questions such as, "Do you know of any person who has died from a smoking related disease, or do you know of someone who is at this time ill through smoking?" "What do your family and friends think of you smoking?" "Have you had any warning signs that your own health is suffering?" "Has your doctor mentioned your smoking?"

Much of the time, the answers to all these questions and more will emerge as the client begins to talk frankly, perhaps for the first time in his/her life, about the habit and what he/she knows to be the dangers and the social consequences.

In therapy, we use the fears and the aspirations of our clients to their profound good, as we project that danger and fear which is consciously recognized into the subconscious mind where the seat of the habit dwells.

In the foreword of this book, I have mentioned that the scripts contained within should be considered as adaptable. They are not a magic formula which, if incanted in the special circumstance of hypnotic trance, will instantly turn lead into gold. You will learn to utilize the special fears and motivations of your individual clients and build into the framework which is the script effective interventions appropriate to the circumstances present.

For a young woman of childbearing age, the importance of providing a good, rich supply of oxygenated blood clear and free of contaminants has to be a factor that can be used with effect. "Do you really wish to feed your baby on nicotine, arsenic, benzo-pyrene, carbon monoxide, etc."? I am sure that by now you have caught my drift.

As therapists, we see ourselves as members of a caring profession, but that does not mean that we must not use those aspects of smoking which are frightening. Indeed, it is sometimes necessary to show the full horror of what could be and to demonstrate what is eminently possible if the responsibility is not taken by the client for his/her own life and health.

The granny with her grandchildren can be reduced to floods of tears when she is asked in hypnosis to see herself not being allowed to hold her new-born grandchild. Similarly, the father given a suggestion that he is in a room with all his family around him and is instructed to tell them all that he has but a short time left to live, having contracted a smoking-related disease (the disease you have established to be the one he most fears), and to tell them all why. Whose fault it is that he will not be there for them?

We accentuate the guilt and the remorse, not because we are sadistic and take pleasure from the reaction that we invoke, but because we know that emotion is a very powerful driving force. After all, what is it that constitutes memory?

After the guilt and the remorse comes, the congratulations and the confidence-boosting, the sense of achievement and the knowledge that, from this moment forward, they will no longer be dependent on anything other than that which they possessed all along .... confidence and self-esteem generated from within.

When all around is chaos and unpredictable, we humans seek constancy and predictability, and it can be seen that, whatever else is happening and changing outside our control and influence, "a cigarette stays the same". A cigarette is constant, it is predictable, it does provide, at some level, a sense of constancy, and in this way can become a very potent influence. Therein lies the power of the habit.

I cannot emphasize enough the importance of tailoring your presentation of the script of the stop-smoking sessions to each client. Do carefully consider and use his/her fears and aspirations. This means of course, that you listen to what he or she is telling you as well as to what is being said.

I am including here a specimen questionnaire which will provide a basis for the initial interview. Once again, please accept it as a guide only. There are so many questions that could be asked, and so many answers that could be given. Every answer given has meaning that is particular to the person who is answering. To listen and hear really is the key.

Smokers' Questionnaire

Name: .... Age: .... Male/Female: ...... Date: ....

Address: ....

.... Tel: ....

Occupation: ....

Occupational Stressors: ....

....

Partner: .... Children: ....

Conditions within Relationship: ....

....

How many cigarettes etc. smoked per day?: ....

For how long?: ....

Why did you start?:   .... Peer pressure

                    .... Rebelling against authority

                    .... Mother and Father smoked

                    .... To appear more adult

                    .... To appear more sophisticated

                    .... Other

What do you get from smoking?

                    .... It relaxes me

                    .... It helps me to concentrate

                    .... It's an excuse for a break

                    .... It gives me a confidence boost

                    .... It's a prop

                    .... Other

When do you smoke?:   .... On waking

                    .... At breakfast

                    .... With tea

                    .... After meals

                    .... On the telephone

                    .... Whilst driving

                    .... At work

                    .... In bed

                    .... Other

What frightens you about smoking?: ....

....

....

Do you know someone:

(a) who died from smoking related disease? ....

(b) who is ill now? ....

Who is important to you?: ....

WHY?: ....

....

What else is important to you?: ....

....

Has your doctor mentioned your smoking to you?: ....

Have you had any warning signals or symptoms?: ....

Do you have any health problems?: ....

....

How long do you want to live?: .... Why?:......................

Whose responsibility is your health?: ....

What will you be able to do as a non-smoker that you could not do before?: ....

....

What will you do with the money you save?: ....

....

Do you really want to quit?: .... What's stopping you?: ....

....

Observations: ....

....

....

....

....

....

....

....

....

....

Foetal Smokers

For use with expectant mothers, incorporate into Diamond Smoking Script.

Now as you go deep inside, you can be aware that, just as you have eyes that see the world about you, now closed and so relaxed .... you also have an eye which we can call your mind's eye .... and this eye is there for your subconscious to see all of those things which are so important to you now. Your mind's eye is very powerful, and you can allow it now to show you deep within yourself a very special part where something miraculous .... something wonderful .... is occurring .... as you travel now where your perfect subconscious mind takes you .... as you go so very deep within .... you can be aware of a gentle yet powerful connection between your own creative and maternal self with another who is yet to be born .... growing within you. I am now going to count from one to three, and with each count, your mind's eye will show you more clearly .... within your womb .... where your own child even now is growing .... nurtured and loved .... one .... becoming clear .... two .... clearer still .... three .... you can see quite clearly now that growing child within you and you can understand now the special communication that can be experienced now .... here is your child .... nurtured within you .... reliant on you for a rich supply of oxygenated blood full of nutrients, so that it may develop within you and grow healthy and strong, and I know that you can feel that special love now .... that desire to ensure that your baby has nothing less than the best that you can provide .... You eat all of the most nutritious foods .... full of vitamins .... healthy foods .... and you take so much care with what you drink .... aware of caffeine .... of alcohol .... of chemical additives .... their potential to harm your baby .... You determine now to commit yourself to being the best that you can be .... to ensure that your child is supplied with nutrient-rich oxygenated blood, free from contamination .... free from tar .... free from nicotine .... free from ammonia .... from benzo-pyrene .... free from carbon monoxide and from cyanide and from arsenic and from all the harmful and destructive chemicals contained in cigarettes .... And you can tell that child within you now of your love and your commitment to ensure that all is as it should be .... tell that child now .... and hear the voice of your child from deep within that creates a bond that will grow and become so powerful .... and should you wish, you can ask your child whether it will be born a girl or a boy .... and you can ask and be told so much .... so go ahead now while I just stay quiet for a few moments while you speak within privately .... and you can tell me when you are content that all is well .... just say "I am content".

(Wait for response and continue with stop smoking therapy.)

Diamond Smoking Script

Now as you relax, drifting deeper with every word that I speak, the first thing I would like you to know is just how much I appreciate and admire you for the decision you have made to give up once and for all this foul habit.

So many people come here for help with this problem; they say "I have no discipline .... I have no motivation." My answer to all of them is this: .... that person who has no motivation and no self-discipline did not come here today; .... that person is not sitting there, comfortable and relaxed in that chair; that person did not make an appointment, ... did not turn up on time, ... simply stayed where they were, not knowing the difference between where they are now .... and where they want to be. You have all the discipline that you need .... you have all the motivation that you need .... but, what you do not have .... yet .... is self-confidence. The self-confidence that it takes to set out on any journey .... or undertake any task, knowing that you have made all the preparations .... that you are completely prepared in all respects .... believing that you can .... that you will complete your journey or task easily .... quickly and without effort .... the same self-confidence it takes to recognize the signs of success .... just as you recognize now those comfortable hypnotic sensations .... perhaps a heaviness of legs .... or lightness of arms .... those physical signs that allow to you to know that you have moved from one state to another state in a calm and confident way. And in this calm and confident state .... you can offer yourself generous portions of self-confidence .... large helpings of self-esteem .... breathing out self-doubt as you relax even deeper and continue to enjoy the journey towards your goal.

Your conscious mind is fully aware of all of the dangers to health and to life that are the legacy of the tobacco trade; after all, there are enough warnings on television and in the press for all to see, ... there are even warnings from your caring government on the packets that you buy, ... and what about the obscene waste of hard-earned money that smoking signifies? Perhaps here .... now .... it is worthwhile to review the damage that is inflicted by you on your body each time you light up a cigarette.

Fact: .... in this country alone, over 500 people die an early death each day through smoking. Doctors attribute in excess of 450,000 heart attacks each year to smoking .... and although cancer would appear to be the most obvious health hazard .... and it is true that a smoker is 50% more likely to contract cancer .... It can be so easy to say, "It won't happen to me. Cancer happens to other people." Perhaps, then, it is right that we now consider some of the other ways that smoking can damage your health and even life itself.

The heart of a smoker works so much harder, beating up to 10,000 extra beats every day, as it struggles to combat the effects of nicotine .... restricting .... clogging .... closing up the arteries .... increasing blood-pressure as it strives to deliver oxygenated blood so necessary for the function of the vital organs of your body .... the muscles .... the brain.

You have told me that a cigarette helps you to relax .... Now I invite you to review and to question that statement in the light of knowledge that, in addition to the fact that your heart is working so much harder, each time you take cigarette smoke into your lungs, you introduce into your body in excess of 4,000 different chemical compounds, many of them deadly poisons .... none of them in any way beneficial. Your body reacts to these lethal poisons in the same way as when subjected to sheer terror .... the automatic response that we know as the "fight or flight response" is activated .... adrenaline production is elevated .... respiration increases .... blood pressure increases as the body prepares to fight, or to run away from danger. Nicotine .... Tar .... Ammonia .... Benzo-pyrene .... Carbon monoxide .... Arsenic .... Cyanide .. to name just a few, and what about the chemical fertilizers and the insecticides that are sprayed on the growing tobacco crops.... remaining to be included in cigarettes .... now absorbed into the tissues of your body?

Does this sound like relaxation? You know the truth, and this truth now becomes deeply embedded in the subconscious of your mind, not to be denied.

As your heart works harder, your lungs strive to perform their essential function. The inside of the lungs and airways are covered in tiny hair-like projections called scillia, and these become coated with thick sticky tar .... they become brittle and lie flat against the walls of the airways, now unable to perform their function of preventing small particles of dust and infectious matter from entering into the small air spaces where oxygenation of the blood takes place.

The lungs become less efficient as they clog with filth .... the mucus lining of the lungs becomes weakened and the whole body is starved of oxygen. Deprivation of oxygen to the brain can mean that the clear-thinking ability of a smoker is diminished by up to 23%. Smoking impairs your ability to concentrate .... it fogs your mind .. clouds your judgment .... but I don't want you to think about that too much.

Pulmonary emphysema .... chronic bronchitis .... lung cancer .... the coughs and the colds .... so frequent and so difficult to shake off .... the breathlessness that obliges you to use the lift when it would be so easy to use the stairs. The coughing .... the mucus .... the vile taste .... the awful smell now an integral part of you .... so offensive to those who object to your vile habit of smoking. You are intensely aware that you are not welcome in many public places .... theatres .... restaurants .... at work .... at play .... you indulge your habit out of sight .... in secret, ashamed, guilty. The taste and the smell that you have chosen for so long to ignore is now strong .... and from this moment forward you are reminded constantly .... powerfully .... in a manner which cannot be ignored each time that you are reminded of cigarettes.

Tissue which do not receive enough oxygen .... die .... as arteries become constricted and blocked .... arteriosclerosis becomes a word with particular meaning for you, as deprived of oxygen, ... part of you dies .... gangrene .... mortification of the flesh sets in .... and now, to save your life, a leg is surgically removed .... maybe both, or perhaps an arm. What is your quality of life now? Ask yourself right now and tell me clearly *(client's name)*; is this for you?

Heart disease .... stroke .... cancer of the liver .... the throat .... the pancreas .... the kidneys .... the tongue .... breast cancer .... cancer of the uterus .... of the ovaries .... of the testicles .... of the skin .... ulcers .... the list is endless and unforgiving, as the hospitals and modern medicine struggle to cope with the self-imposed destruction of those who are unwilling to accept the responsibility for their own life, their own health and happiness .... to protect and respect the miracle that is their own body.

***

It is a fact that the skin of a smoker ages more rapidly than that of a non-smoker. A fifty-year-old smoker is as old physically as a seventy-year-old non-smoker. Each cigarette reduces life expectancy by 6 minutes .... 20 per day means 2 hours of life that may never be .... but I don't want you to think about that too much.

The sexual prowess and potency of a smoker will diminish more rapidly with age than that of a non-smoker, and you can know that you can give so much more in that way by ensuring that you are fitter, more virile .... more attractive .... and that means non-smoker. Each smoker inhales just 15% of the smoke from their cigarette, the remainder goes directly into the atmosphere that we all have to breathe. Those whom you love and care for must also breathe the air that a smoker poisons. Perhaps you can agree with me that one very good reason for quitting this disgusting habit is that, through your excellent example, you may influence someone younger against taking up the habit. Just think of how much you could achieve, if just one young person was prevented from taking up the habit .... think of all the misery and the pain that could be prevented if that disgusting and costly mistake were avoided.

✗MISS

Now (*client's name*), please take a deep breath, and, as you release all of the air from your lungs, relax and go deeper .... as you allow your mind to show you yourself in a room .... all around you here are those you love and care for, and who love and care for you .... all who celebrate your decision to give up smoking and take the responsibility for your own health .... your own life .... to become your own person.

As you go deeper now, see them all before you, gathered here as you listen to the sound of my voice and the truth that is so important to you now. They are all here, they have come from far and near .... (*give names of significant people*) .... all have come because you have something to tell them .... a dreadful truth .... Your doctor has told you that you have contracted cancer and that you have but a short time to live, soon you will be gone .... You will be dead before your time, all because you ignored all the good advice, the wishes of those who wanted so much for you to give up smoking .... you made the choice .... a choice to die, and soon you will not be there for them who rely on you to be a part of their life.

You refused to accept the responsibility for your own health and for your own life, and now the immune system that you have relied on without consideration for so long to repair the ravages that you have inflicted upon your body, has given up .... overwhelmed .... defeated .... now you will die before your time and you must tell all here that terrible truth .... and tell them why .... and tell them who is responsible. Go ahead now and as you tell them, see their faces .... see the shock, the horror, the disbelief .... and then the anger .... the grief. And how do you feel?

An insidious habit has destroyed all .... your health, your life, wasted enormous amounts of money, enriching those few who would benefit without conscience or regard for the misery they purvey, selling in attractive packaging what you know to be no less than lethal poison.

Now feel the guilt .... the guilt that has for so long been repressed and ignored each time you lit up a cigarette .... Now feel it strongly .... so strong and powerful .... that feeling of shame when sneaking away to indulge in that filthy destructive habit away from friends and colleagues who are offended by it.

See ashtrays overflowing with stale and stinking cigarette butts .... burn holes in furnishings and in clothes..... stained paintwork and ceilings, brown and dingy..... intensely aware now of the smell that lingers and of the taste that disgusts you now each time you are reminded of cigarettes. And now remind yourself of your commitment, your promise to yourself .... that commitment now growing strong and powerful .... intense now .... your desire to pollute your mouth .... your body..... has gone completely .... and your subconscious mind helps you now with new and powerful responses and your desire to smoke has gone .... vanished completely, replaced with feelings of justifiable pride and deep personal satisfaction .... feelings of real and significant accomplishment.

Each day you feel stronger .... more alive .... your confidence and good feelings about yourself expand and grow .... become powerful .... no longer do you offend those about you with stinking tobacco-laden breath, stained teeth and reeking clothes and hair .... you are fitter, healthier, more attractive .... more alive.

As a non-smoker, you continue to enjoy a longer and healthier sex life and give so much more in that way. You experience pleasure that you are still capable of, long after the sexual prowess of a smoker of your age has failed them. No longer do you look for self-confidence .... for self-esteem .... for ways of coping with problems .... in packets of cigarettes .... You are aware that good feelings about yourself and your life come from deep within .... not from sticks of poisonous weed, false promises and illusions. There is no room for illusion in your life.

You see yourself now as a confident and self-assured non-smoker .... proud of your achievement .... those around you who continue to smoke do not concern you .... You wish for them the same good feelings and the freedom that you now experience .... the new-found reality that is life without the need or desire for the destructive effects of cigarettes. To them you express a gentle understanding indifference, coupled with your own firm resolve as you express and assert yourself always as that person who has no need or desire for cigarettes.

You can be intensely aware of the pride in your achievement each time you refuse cigarettes, and should you ever, through mistake or childish impulse, ever put a cigarette or tobacco product to your lips ever again .... your subconscious mind will remind you in a powerful and unmistakable way .... of the nauseating smell, of the vile, disgusting taste, and of the guilt that attends each and every cigarette .... You will be reminded of your responsibility that cannot be passed to any other .... your health .... your life .... your body .... your commitment to yourself and those who love and care for you and who rely on you to be there.

***

Now you may decide to quit smoking right now .... or perhaps you may decide that later on today is a good time for you .... perhaps you may quit after lunch .... after dinner .... or just before you go to bed. Now I would prefer that you stop smoking immediately, but it's entirely up to you to discover .... today the right time for you to free yourself forever from smoking .... aware that your subconscious mind knows what to do for you, thinking with an awareness of things thought .... those things that are done automatically for you .... driving your car .... having no need or desire to smoke .... speaking on the telephone .... having no need or desire to smoke

.... enjoying all those things that you have done before, and more, as that person who has lost any need or desire to smoke .... that person that now takes the full responsibility for life .... for health and happiness, and you can congratulate yourself right now on your excellent achievement, ... experience now the feeling of deep personal satisfaction as your confidence and your self-esteem grow and expand .... as your health and fitness improve with each and every new day .... that problem finally resolved.

***

And now as you feel so good about yourself, you can imagine that on a table in front of you now is a packet of those cigarettes that you used to smoke .... that you have wasted so much upon. Now see a strong wind blowing .... a powerful wind and see that wind blowing stronger and stronger .... blowing a gale now .... and see that powerful, cleansing wind scattering that packet of cigarettes and see the foul contents of the packet disintegrating and being swept away by that wind as it blows away each and every trace and every memory of that tobacco .... further .... further .... away into infinity, and with it every small desire to pollute your own body.

And when you can see that cleansing wind has done its work and all traces and memory of that tobacco have gone completely .... the wind drops and peace .... calm and tranquillity return completely now .... you see yourself clearly now as a natural non-smoker and you can tell me clearly .... "I am now a non-smoker".

(Wait for response)

That's good .... a very special part of you remembers clearly now the vile taste and the noxious odour of tobacco .... strong and intense .... and, should you ever through accident or childish, irresponsible impulse ever put a cigarette or tobacco product to your lips again, that part will provide you with an instant and disgusting reminder that you are a non-smoker .... responsible and proud. You are your own person.

Life-Style Junction

You stopped smoking because you made a promise to yourself .... you made a commitment .... you made a decision .... but you know, it is more than that. What this all narrows down to is one very simple premise .... on this path of life you have been faced with a choice .... the choice that you are faced with is a junction on the road, a fork on the road of life, and a choice.

Of course you can continue down that same old road .... live your life with the smell, the cough, the phlegm and the colds that are so frequent and never seem to go away .... the shortness of breath, the guilt and the fear .... Of course you can continue living your life enslaved by packets of cigarettes .... or at this fork in the road .... this junction .... you can choose to turn off the beaten track .... to take that turning off to the right .... onto a new road of opportunity .... to continue living your life in a new and powerfully positive and exciting way .... healthy .... strong .... vital .... vibrant .... powerfully alive and free from the bonds and chains that are cigarettes .... You are at that fork in the road right now .... now you must make that choice, and I want you to tell me which road do you intend to take from here?

(Pause for reply)

Now tell me what that road looks like .... what do you see?

Repeat and affirm client's description of the road, emphasizing the cleanness and the freshness of the air, the perfume of flowers and the taste of food, fitness and health etc., etc.

Affirmation Of Inner Self

This script can be used at any time to allow the client the opportunity to experience something pleasant and positive.

And now, as you allow that trance to continue and to deepen even more, I wonder how much more comfortable and tranquil you really can become .... aware now perhaps of that pleasant heaviness of arms .... of legs .... of the whole body, that just seems to be there but then perhaps some way off from here .... there in that chair resting .... comfortable .... while the conscious mind continues to drift and allow the subconscious more and more of the responsibility for allowing that awareness of just how little you need to concern yourself about things that are of little moment.

It can happen if you wish .... that your subconscious mind can allow you an opportunity to experience those things which are pleasant and positive .... to surprise you perhaps with a pleasant thought .... a long forgotten memory of a happy event .... even a taste or a fragrance .... a warm and all-embracing feeling of being at one with yourself .... a brilliant colour that will suddenly evoke that feeling .... that memory .... that pleasant feeling of how wonderful it is to be alive to experience those moments that really do stand out .... wonderful times of pleasant experience .... and you can know then that you really do not need to know just how your subconscious mind knows how to do that for you in that way .... simply take the moment, and bask in the light of that revelation .... as your subconscious mind opens up .... allowing that inner voice and that creative and unique part of you to give to you that gift .... that feeling that will allow you to understand even more.

Weight On The Mind

One of the problems which so many people present to a hypnothera-pist is that of weight. Of course, there are so many considerations to take into account when dealing with these unhappy people who feel so bad about themselves.

Overeating is so often just a symptom of the underlying problem, and the phrase "weight on the mind" can seem so very appropriate.

For the person who is overweight, the problem of self-image is extremely acute, and it can be argued that the dictates of fashion can be a powerful factor in shaping the image of self which is so important and so powerful.

We need to ask why this person is compelled to overeat when it really does make him/her miserable. Can it be that they wish to make themselves unattractive to the opposite sex in order to avoid having to form relationships?

Is the food eaten as a substitute for love and affection missing in that person's life? Perhaps it is just a habit by the manner in which the parents encouraged the child to eat up everything on the plate. "Eat it all up now. Think of all the starving children in Africa"; powerful incantations that can stay with us into adult life. Isn't this logic a little strange though, that, by eating much more food than we actually need, we can compensate for the fact of another's hunger? The concept of waste can be a powerful factor. For many of us, our parents will have experienced times of shortage and hardship which in these modern times cannot really be appreciated. The message "waste not, want not" is passed through the generations, and the habit passed on from parent to child. I have a new message which I consider much more appropriate and effective: "You can waste food in the bin, or you can waste it on your waist .... waste to waist."

It is important that the therapist considers carefully the course of intervention that will be used to help the overweight client. Investigate thoroughly the background of the client, and if necessary use analysis to determine the true motivations before wading in with suggestion therapy which could prove inappropriate.

Personally, I favour an approach using the "six-step reframe" at the first appointment, and then gauging the response of the client during the following week. At the second appointment, it will be easier to determine the course that the therapy should then take. The fact is, there is no easy answer that will apply in all cases. Each one will be different, and must be treated in a manner which is well-considered.

The scripts provided for weight therapy should always be used taking account of the person, and only the therapist can make the decision as to the advisability of a particular approach.

Weight - What I Tell 'Em

The following paragraphs are a condensation of the talks that I give to groups of people who are interested in losing weight. I include it, because I believe that it helps to be able to speak to clients with some authority, thereby gaining their confidence. You may disagree with some of the content. That's fine. Wouldn't it be a dreary old world if nobody questioned or put forward new thoughts and ideas? In this profession, the discussion of old and new ideas and strategies can only help us all to be the best therapists that we can, and in that way we serve those who need us to the best of our ability.

Eating For Life

We all have to eat. Marvellous as our bodies are, they are in fact very complex machines which require fuel in order to function. We require energy in order to be active and, in the same way a car burns either petrol or diesel as fuel, we 'burn' food.

When our car is burning too much fuel, how quick we are to tackle the problem. After all, it costs money to fill the tank. Excessive fuel consumption means that the engine is consuming too much for the amount of power that it returns, and so down goes the M.P.G.. The excess fuel cannot be burned efficiently, and so it ends up as thick carbon deposits which gum up the works and reduce the effectiveness of the engine. The life of the engine will be reduced if the problem is not attended to quickly.

In the same way, if we overload our engine with more food than it needs and/or use the wrong types of fuel, then our performance will be affected. We will build up deposits of unburned fuel in the form of body fat and, of course, the efficiency and the life expectancy will be reduced as we place extra loading upon it.

I have no intention of laying out a specific and rigid diet. In all probability, you will have tried most of the clever diets; the exotic and different ways of losing excess pounds, and by now you will have realized that the only thing you will lose permanently is money paid out for the marvellous products which you feed yourself with in order to lose weight. What I will outline for you is a basis on which you can take control of your own eating habits and the responsibility for your own health and well-being.

First we have to address our eating habits and be honest with ourselves. When do we eat, where do we eat and how do we eat? Why do we eat?

Do you chew your food thoroughly, savouring each mouthful, or make a race of it, cramming in as much as possible in a short time?

Do you eat on the run? Do you reward yourself with food? Do you pacify yourself, in times of trouble and stress, with food? Do you eat snacks between your main meals?   Do you reward your children with food? Do you give your children a snack so that you too can enjoy a treat?

An extremely important question that you must ask yourself is: "Do I really want to lose weight?", and if the answer is "Yes", then "Why?" Make sure that what you are doing is for you and your self-esteem and not a fad of convention. You should be happy with yourself and your decisions.

Okay, now we get down to a plan of action that is going to achieve what you want for yourself. Set yourself attainable goals and believe always that you can and you will do this for yourself. First I want you to take a good look at when you eat and where you eat. If you do not eat at set times during the day, then right now resolve to eat at a time which you will designate as a mealtime. Make it a mealtime for all the family as much as is possible.

Where do you eat? If you find yourself, as so many do these days, sitting down in front of the television with a tray upon your lap, then I want you never to do that again. Eat at the table and, when you eat, concentrate on what you are doing. You do not eat while doing other things. You now eat slowly, chew your food properly and savour the taste and the texture, amazed at how much more enjoyment you will get from mealtimes if you take the time to taste your food.

When you feel hunger, what in fact is happening is that a tiny sensor at the base of the brain, called the hypothalamus, is sending a message to let you know that it is time to eat. About 20 minutes after it has told you that you need to eat, it then sends another message telling you that it is satisfied, and the feelings associated with hunger subside. Just think now of all the times when you felt hungry and, even though you did not eat, the hunger pangs just went away. This is important for you to know, because from this moment forward you are aware that it is not how much you eat during that twenty minutes that will satisfy the feelings of hunger at all. The hypothalamus will allow you to eat as much or as little as possible in that twenty minutes before sending the exact same message of satisfaction. Crazy but true!

As you begin to lose weight, it will be necessary for you to drink plenty. It doesn't matter too much what you drink, as long as it is not alcohol, which has much in the way of calories but next to nought in the way of nutrition. Drinks with high sugar content must be avoided. If you decide that you can stick to mineral or spa water then that is fine, as is tea and coffee without sugar. The more you drink, the more you will need to go to the bathroom and in a very natural manner flush away the toxins that are stored in the body fats.

Now for some of the more serious don'ts: there are of course foods which are extremely non-beneficial in our quest for the slim and attractive body that is hidden within those extra pounds. White flour products are definitely bad news: these include cakes and pies, white bread, biscuits, sausage rolls and so on. White, refined flour. Burn this now into your mind and resolve to ensure that you will ever be on your guard to ensure that you do not buy or bake foods with white, refined flour. Bread made with wholemeal flour is fine, and will prove a very potent weapon in your fight to retain the slim and elegant you that you are going to be. Make a list of all of the white flour products that you can think of. Now have a look in your cupboards to see how many of these products are lurking there. Now do the same for products made with whole-meal flour and see how much real choice you have in designing a healthy eating regime for yourself.

Many dairy products are to be avoided. Think now of the contents of the dairy cabinet at your supermarket and you will find it easy, with just a little care, to determine which of those products have a lower fat content. Low-fat spreads and cheeses, yoghurts and many other treats can be found with low fat contents. Why, they even make low-fat ice cream these days. It will surprise you, too, how the once mundane task of getting in the weekly shopping can now prove to be an interesting experience. You will enjoy the quest for those foods which are healthy and beneficial, and surprise, surprise, the tills will not ring so loudly either.

No longer will you experience that pang of guilt, when you choose those foods which you know are not part of your healthy eating plan. Being slim will improve your love-life! There, that grabbed your attention, did it not? If you feel more attractive, then you will project that feeling in your love-making, and that can be much more exciting that munching on a cream bun. Am I right?

As you begin to lose the weight that has been with you for so long, you will feel better about yourself, more confident and more energetic, no longer having to carry around with you that excess fat. As you feel better, you will become more determined to increase that feeling of well-being, more motivated to become the person who is in control, who has the body that you want and that you deserve.

Fruit and vegetables become a regular part of your daily diet. Why not ensure that there is fruit, celery and carrot, etc, in the fridge, cut up into snack sized pieces? Do not allow yourself to become obsessed with foods that you cannot have. It does not pay to be too hard on yourself and, if you do make a slip, just accept that you are human and then carry on with your eating plan. Do not treat any food as taboo. You are fully aware of what is good and what is not, and you are also aware of whose responsibility it is to look after your body and of how good you feel as you move ever closer to your goal.

Diamond Weight Control

First (*client's name*), I would like you to know how much I appreciate and admire you for the decision that you have taken, to take on for yourself fully the responsibility for your own life .... to respect and protect your own body.

It is with our body that we enjoy the good things of life ... and today you decided that it is time to take the action that you need to take .... to change those ways of doing things in that way .... the right way for you.

You are aware of your desire to eat good food .... you are aware that your body needs food to remain healthy .... and you are also aware that there are foods which are good and nutritious, and that there are foods which can do you harm .... make you fat ... making you feel sad .... feel very guilty and then very angry .... and then these negative emotions harm you also.

Now that you have taken your decision to lose weight .... and to respect your own body .... you will be pleasantly surprised at how easily you will be able to achieve your goal .... a slim and healthy, attractive body.

I wonder if you can imagine, just how many people come here to ask me for help with this problem or that .... who will tell me that they do not have the drive or the determination to succeed .... to make those changes for themselves which are necessary to improve the quality of their life. .... I tell all of those people .... the person who has no drive, did not make an appointment .... that person who has no determination did not arrive on time if at all .... and that person who has no vision is not sitting there in that chair so relaxed and so comfortable .... you have all that you need to do all of those things and to achieve your worthwhile goals .... but there is just one thing that you do not have, that you will take with you when you leave here today .... that is confidence .... confidence that you recognise now .... of the kind it takes to tackle any task .... or set out on a journey knowing that you have done all that is required .... made all arrangements .... certain that you will complete the task or journey safely .... quickly and without fuss .... just as you recognise now those signs of success in achieving a wonderfully relaxed and comfortable state .... sensing a gentle connection with your perfect inner self that tells you that you can .... you will .... that you have all of the confidence that you need .... recognising too those heavy, comfortable feelings as your whole body relaxes and your mind relaxes deeper and deeper with each word that I speak.

I am reminded now of a man who built himself a fine house .... a house that he designed himself .... built on a plot of land right on the edge of town, with fantastic views over rolling hills and valleys to the sea. He had a dream of building this house for many years and spent so many long hours poring over the drawings .... imagining himself in that house .... enjoying the garden .... the pool .... planning how he would furnish it and decorate it. Then came the day when his hard work and his planning came to fruition .... and he bought the plot of land .... and he built that house just as he dreamed it .... furnished it .... decorated it exactly how he wanted it. He married his true love, and I wonder if you can know how proud he felt as he carried his new bride over the threshold of that dream home. He spent many hours in that house .... for he worked from home in an office that he had incorporated in the plans ..... and as he worked, his new wife busied herself around the house in the way that a wife does to make a house a home. .... Neither of them noticed at first the feelings of lethargy .... the constant headaches that never seemed to ease ..... putting it down to working too hard at ensuring that their home and their life was as perfect as could be. They consulted their doctor and he gave them pills and potions, but to no avail .... they never seemed to feel any better .... feeling that their health was just fading away .... but they did have a beautiful home. It was over two years before they got round to taking a holiday .... jetting off to the delights of foreign lands .... and they were both amazed, that after just a few days .... all the feelings of lethargy ..... the headaches .... just disappeared: .... they were their old selves once again.

On their return .... the husband made some enquiries .... speaking to some of the local farmers, and was amazed to discover that the land he had built his house upon was contaminated .... an old dumping ground .... He called in an expert and was told that poisonous chemicals were present in the soil .... and gases were seeping from the ground poisoning his house and poisoning both him and his wife. It took just a day for him to get out of that house .... for he knew that his health and that of those he loved were more important than any house .... no matter how much he had wanted it.

Nobody likes to be told what to do .... and if I were able to tell you what to do .... then you would have no need at all to be here today .... you would simply call me on the 'phone and say .... "*(therapist's name)*, I would like to lose weight and be able to wear the clothes that I would like to wear .... in a size .... *(desired dress size)*," .... and I would say to you ...."*(client's name)*, ... that's a great idea .... stop overeating and eating those foods that are unhealthy and fattening and instead eat only those foods which are healthy and non-fattening .... do it right now." .... But nobody likes to be told what to do .... so I wouldn't say to you that overeating and eating those foods which are unhealthy and which make you fat .... are 's dangerous .... They are dangerous and will prevent you from having the body that you desire .... the body that you are entitled to .... the body that you deserve .... slim and firm and beautiful .... and I needn't tell you that you will get no pleasure from butter and cheese .... or from any dairy products that are so high in fat content and so high in calories .... fattening and unhealthy foods .... you will get no pleasure from overeating .... but you will become aware of feelings of great pride and accomplishment when you choose foods that are healthy and non-fattening. I need never say to you that overeating .... unhealthy and fattening foods is no substitute for lack of adequate stimulation in your life .... or for love that you need and are entitled to have .... I need never tell you that you do not need to eat more food than is necessary to maintain your body at the weight that will allow you to wear the clothes that you choose in a size *(desired dress size)* .... weighing a comfortable slim and lovely .... *(target weight)*. But one thing I will say to you .... is that controlling your eating is not something that you will not find easy .... and when you leave here today you will no longer be that person who overeats and eats those foods which are unhealthy and fattening ..... you know that you have a desire for foods like biscuits .... butter .... cheese .... cakes .... sweet things with lots of sugar .... and you know that nobody can talk you out of it .... But what you know now .... that you didn't before .... is that you also have an enormous amount of NO DESIRE .... and you can get to know this place of ... NO DESIRE .... as it expands and reaches deeper and deeper and the feelings of .... NO DESIRE .... can reach even deeper .... and the time of .... NO DESIRE .... grow longer and longer .... and no way is easier than this.

That house was a lovely dream, but the price was just too much to pay .... and it's good to finally resolve those feelings and to just let go .... not needing to know how the unconscious mind knows what to do for you .... thinking with an awareness of things .... thoughts .... without the need to know those things that are done automatically .... You know what to do ✗ now I would prefer that you stop overeating .... and eating unhealthy and fattening foods right away .... immediately .... but it's entirely up to you to discover the time .... today .... the best time and the best way for you .... some people wait an hour .... some wait until they have used up stocks of food at home .... and then some stop entirely before they go to bed .... Now I'd prefer that you stop right now .... immediately .... but it's entirely up to you to choose a time today when you free yourself forever from this unhealthy and fattening habit forever.

We have all suffered the loss of some one that we love .... or something or situation that we value .... and we can be aware that gone is an important part of our life.

You can be aware right now of the responsibility that you have towards those who love you and care for you .... who you love and care for .... special people who rely on you to be there for them .... the responsibility that is yours and yours alone to ensure that those people will not be faced with the loss of that person .... whom they love and treasure .... responsibility to ensure that you live a healthy and long life .... respecting and protecting your body .... cherishing your gift of life .... that person eating just what you need .... eating foods which are healthy and in the right amounts and at the right times.

You can waste food .... you can waste it .... put it into the bin .... or you can waste food on your waist .... waste to waist .... I wonder what you will prefer. Whenever you see those foods which are unhealthy .... foods which will pile on the pounds .... you will be reminded in a manner that is instant and powerful as your subconscious mind helps you .... reminds you of your commitment with images of you that have distressed you and those feelings of guilt and sadness that attend that fat, overweight person that you used to be. You accept now without reservation the total responsibility for your own health .... your own life .... your own happiness .... You are now your own person .... proud and confident .... You see yourself always as that person in control of her life .... slim, lithe and lovely .... that problem finally resolved.

(Go to trance termination)

"Swish Pattern" .... Weight Loss

First, establish with your client the weight he/she wishes to be, dress size etc.

Establish goals. Establish that the subconscious is very specific and that, if the goal is a realistic one, then it will happen.

Diets: Deprivation .... the basic instinct of the subconscious is survival, and deprivation does not fit in with that concept. Comfortable, however, does fit .... it's nice to be comfortable.

Imagine now that you are in a restaurant watching some slim people looking through the menu. What are they doing? .... mentally they are tasting the food .... visualizing how it will look served on the plate .... what they are not thinking about is how comfortable they will feel .... food remains in the stomach for up to four hours and it is important to know how comfortable that will feel.

Now what I want you to be thinking about is yourself .... *(desired weight loss)* .... think about how good you will feel about yourself .... how good you will look .... what you are wearing .... and what your friends and family will think about how good you look .... but I don't want you to think about that too much.

Now we will do some hypnosis and during the course of this therapy which is all for your benefit and, only with your approval, I will need at times to touch your hands .... your forehead .... and then your knee .... I'm telling you this so there is no reason for you to be surprised, and my touch will relax you deeper. Just visualize how you will feel .... lighter .... just how does that feel?
Induction for hypnosis ....

Now *(client's name)*, I want you to go to a special and very pleasant memory of yours .... in the past .... a memory of importance .... of significance to you. There may be a few, but your subconscious mind will understand and know exactly which one is of importance to you now .... of significance to you now .... and unconsciously you know it is of value to you now .... you know as it selects itself .... as you experience those successful feelings .... of importance .... of significance to you now. For you know that the answers come from that memory held way back then. And now go deeper

Roger P. Allen

and as you drift down deeper and deeper now .... I know that I really don't have to tell you that the deeper, you go the better you feel .... and the better you feel, the deeper you go.

And now in your mind .... in your imagination .... I want you to go to a special room .... a special room of belief and of capability .... in this room you will see that there is only one piece of furniture .... that is a television set .... now you can speak to me but you cannot wake .... when you see it .... just say "yes".

That's good .... now what I would like you to do is to put onto the blank screen of that television .... all of that extra weight that you have .... that you want to lose .... put it all up there on that screen .... all of those extra fat cells .... perhaps you can see them as pinkish in colour .... perhaps orangey .... all piled up as a fatty mass .... Now put into the picture just how uncomfortable you feel when you overeat .... Now put into the picture what your family and friends think when you overeat .... now all of the reasons that you have for your need to overeat .... be it lack of love .... unhappiness .... whatever those reasons your subconscious mind knows exactly what is meant here .... just put it all there on that screen. Now put onto that screen all of the damage that overeating does .... all that cholesterol .... high blood pressure .... breathlessness .... the danger of heart attack and stroke .... that uncomfortable feeling when you overeat and also that feeling of guilt and of shame .... shame that you are not taking on the responsibility for your own health and well being .... carrying all of that extra weight .... When you have that picture really clearly in your mind say "yes". *(When the client says "yes" continue.)* .... I now want you to store this picture somewhere convenient in your mind because we will need it later ....

Okay *(client's name)* .... that's good .... now I want you to see another picture there on that screen .... a smaller, inset picture in the top right of the screen .... make this picture one of *(client's name)* now having lost that extra weight *(target weight loss)*, lighter in a dress size *(target size)* .... notice how good she feels .... how she looks .... that feeling of confidence .... increased self-esteem .... happier .... more alive .... lighter in all ways .... *(client's name)* taking care of herself .... and with that feeling of huge optimism.

Now I want you to give *(client's name)* in this picture, on a scale of one to ten .... for confidence .... ten .... for self-esteem .... ten .... give her a score of ten for self-respect.

This is the *(client's name)* who eats only when her appetite says she is hungry .... the *(client's name)* who stops eating when her appetite tells that it is right .... a friend of her appetite .... who is aware that on her tongue are 26,000 taste buds, and when she puts food into her mouth they will very quickly become satisfied .... who chews her food slowly and thoroughly and carefully until her appetite is satisfied .... the *(client's name)* who is fully aware that any more food than is enough to satisfy her appetite .... is waste .... and that waste can either be wasted in the bin .... or wasted on her waist .... waste to waist.

Now in a moment as you watch the screen .... you will hear me say the word "Swish" .... and you can make that small picture grow .... spread across the screen .... that picture of the new you. You will do this very fast and you will do this five time as this is how the subconscious learns .... "SWISH" .... erasing all of those old eating habits .... SWISHING .... erasing all of that extra weight .... all of that discomfort .... that feeling of guilt .... of shame .... until that picture fills the screen eliminating completely that old picture .... filling the screen with that new *(client's name)*.

Now make the screen go blank and put back the old picture and notice what is different about it .... put back the inset picture in the top right corner of the screen .... and now "SWISH" .... again .... "SWISHING" .... erasing .... that old *(client's name)* .... eliminating that excess weight .... "SWISHING" erasing all of those feeling of discomfort .... of lack of confidence .... eliminating those feelings of guilt .... all of those bad eating habits .... all of those negative feelings erased and eliminated as the new *(client's name)* fills the screen completely now.

Now make the screen go blank .... put back the old picture on the screen .... notice what's different .... look at the colour now and tell me what is different about that picture.

(Give client time to tell you what is different .... and then ....)

Now .... "SWISH" again .... *(repeat sequence)*

Now walk over to that television set and turn up the colour .... turn it up as high as it will go .... Now "SWISH" again .... *(repeat sequence)*

Now make the screen go blank .... and put on it now all that remains of that old picture .... the small remains .... the dregs of that old picture .... the smallest traces .... and then "SWISH" again .... erasing all that remains of that old picture .... all that remains of those old eating habits .... those bad feelings .... eliminating completely all of that extra weight .... those feelings of discomfort .... as the new and exciting *(client's name)* fills the screen completely now .... see the new and so confident *(client's name)* .... lighter *(client's name)* .... filling that screen completely now in full and glorious colour .... And now let those wonderful feelings expand and grow now .... *(Anchor good feelings .... touch knee with firm pressure for approximately 10 to 15 seconds.)*

Now step into that picture .... into that TV set, and try out that new body .... that slim and lovely *(client's name)* .... *(desired weight loss)* lighter .... striding out now happy .... smiling .... looking absolutely wonderful .... wearing a beautiful new dress .... size *(target size)* .... walk about now and experience fully that comfort .... that confidence, that self-esteem .... proud now .... slim and attractive ....lithe and lovely .... enjoy that experience and become familiar with the new *(client's name)*.

Now go forward in time .... *(client's name)*, ... *(target loss)* lighter .... wearing that dress in a size *(target size)* .... now a date will flash as your subconscious chooses one that is significant and appropriate .... tell me what is that date? Are you satisfied with that date .... you will be happy to be *(target weight loss)* lighter on .... *(date given)*.

Okay .... now *(client's name)* .... please take a deep breath and go deep inside and try .... try in vain to have that same problem .... It was a terrible problem wasn't it? .... You want to make those changes about you .... think about those changes now .... in the future as you look back and think about it now .... to make that change now for yourself, so that you could stop having that problem now and see yourself now.

Do you like the way that you look? Just look back at yourself having made that change now .... and you will, will you not?

"Swish Pattern" originated by Richard Bandler, 1982

Physical Dissociation

And when your thoughts begin to travel faster than your body can keep up with .... you can re-discover how the mind can travel so far and so fast .... and you can wonder about things that exist in the universe .... the size of the mighty ocean .... the age of the huge trees that fill the sky .... and the number of stars in the night sky .... things that you have wondered about from time to time .... and you can let your mind float freely in that place that you find yourself drawn to .... while your body remains here .... comfortably here .... there is no need to disturb it .... no need to allow it to hold you back .... You can just enjoy the freedom of letting your mind float freely .... to the places that you most enjoy .... and while your mind is there .... and your body is here .... it can be so comforting to know that your body is here .... waiting comfortably .... patiently for as long as you'd like it to float freely without having to notice it .... because your mind can go anywhere that it wants to go.

Amnesia

And as your mind continues to relax .... each breath soothing you .... I wonder how much attention you have paid to the different thoughts floating through your mind .... Your mind can be so active as it relaxes .... and then you can realise how difficult it is to remember .... what I was talking about exactly seven minutes ago .... and you could try to remember what I was saying nine minutes ago .... or what you were thinking four minutes ago .... but doesn't it seem like just too much work .... to try to remember .... it takes more effort than it's worth .... so much easier to allow yourself to relax comfortably .... knowing that you don't have to remember when it really is too much work .... too much effort to bother making ....

Confusion Technique To Facilitate Amnesia

And now that you have had the opportunity to discover new possibilities .... while you can learn from past experiences .... your conscious mind can begin to wonder how it will know which things to remember .... and which things only your subconscious need know .... and then you can remember to forget .... or you may choose to forget to remember .... Your memory of forgetting forgets what it has forgotten .... but you can only forget what you have forgotten when you realise it's too difficult to remember anyway .... and then you can forget all the confusion .... and relax even more deeply than before ....

Coping With Abreaction

When a client experiences the emotions that are attached to long-repressed memories, the event can be extremely dramatic and to a degree quite daunting for the therapist. The importance of the therapist's remaining calm and reassuring is paramount as he/she continues to speak to the client in a voice which is calming and confident.

Explain to the client that the event being experienced is of importance and that there is no need to fear it, as it is but a memory. Initially it was frightening but, having survived the original event, there is no question of its having any power to harm ever again. Now, in the light of conscious awareness, it has lost entirely its power to hurt.

Before initiating a regression session with a client, I make a provision, for example, of suggesting that, if I place my hand on his/her forehead, then he/she will immediately return to the place of safety that has been provided before the regression. This can be a garden, or a beach, a familiar room, etc.. It matters not, as long as it is a place where the client can feel safe and secure.

Having calmed the situation and restored the client to a relaxed state, I will then invite the client to return to the same scenario which frightened him/her so much. The difference, however, is that first I explain the importance of reviewing the event in order that it can be finally resolved, and a more beneficial perspective formed.

The use of visualization can include dissociative techniques - perhaps a video of the event, suggesting to the client that he/she has a remote control with which the video can be run, stopped, backed up, freeze-framed or run forward. The more control that can be suggested, the more comfortable the client will feel, and in this way he/she will feel in control over the past problem area.

Approach the situation by degrees, perhaps allowing just the sound of someone speaking about the event, or perhaps looking at the scene from far away. As he/she draws nearer, the event can be run through without the client actually in the picture at first, then little by little the scene can be added to at a comfortable pace, including the introduction of the client into the scenario.

"And now that you do know what is really occurring there .... you are able to see yourself very clearly in that place at that time .... on the count of three you will be there at that place and at that time".

There are so many ways that this situation can be approached, limited only by the imagination and expertise of the therapist. You will be there to determine how you will need to tailor your approach in a professional and reassuring manner.

"I know and you know too that this event at this time and place is very important and significant to you .... and I would like you to take me along with you as you re-experience now the whole event .... but because I am not able to see or hear what is happening .... or know about your feelings and emotions .... please help me by telling me what is happening .... and how you are feeling .... there is nothing here that can harm you and I want you to know that I am with you here and you are quite safe".

Calm is the key, with the understanding that no harm can come to your client here as he/she releases what is after all emotion that has been contained harmfully for so long. The abreaction is a release and to you, the therapist, the most potent indicator that significant progress is occurring. A large box of man-sized tissues is a must for every consulting room.

Audio & Videotape Therapy

I expect that I am one among many who use pre-recorded audio-tapes with my clients. I consider that they are useful in compounding and reinforcing the content of therapeutic sessions, but would question their value without the planned and considered intervention tailored individually to each client.

I would certainly raise an eyebrow at some therapists' use of taped inductions and suggestion therapy sessions. My argument in this case would be that each and every client is unique, and the valuable and personal utilization of events during the induction and therapy will be lost as the opportunity is missed. "And as you clear

your throat, I wonder if you can notice how much more comfortable you become now with each breath that you take," *and* "You can hear the telephone ringing now, and know that it does not concern you; each ring is but a signal for you to go deeper still."

I explain to my clients that the tapes that I supply are to reinforce what happens in the consulting room and that they will most certainly help, provided that the instructions I give are followed in their use. The suggestion, "If you do this, you will be helped", *is obviously important as it affirms to the client that listening to the tapes will be of value and so he/she will benefit.*

Providing a client with a tape is in effect "compounding". "As you listen to the tape you will become aware of a new confidence." *In the same way, we suggest to a client,* "As your left arm grows heavier, then so the right arm will become lighter and you may be aware of how heavy that heavy arm is now". *It is all suggestion and acceptance by the client.*

Much has been said by others more learned than me, certainly more willing to express their views and expose them to public scrutiny, regarding the "placebo" effect. The fact that we, as therapists, do what we do by suggestion and are effective through the compliance of our clients would suggest that the placebo element is not to be denied. In my engineering days, there was a generally accepted premise: "If it's not broke, don't fix it." *I would suggest that this can be reasonably applied to any arguments that follow this direction.*

Providing a person with a "medicine" that is nothing more than perhaps a sugar solution and telling them with authority, "Drink this and you will feel better", can easily be equated with suggestion therapy. Placebo maybe, but what the hell? If it works, if it proves beneficial to those who come to us seeking help, then call it what you will, but use it and you will experience the gratitude of those who, maybe because they have believed that they will be helped, are helped. Therefore you have helped them, and do not need to justify something of whose immense value you are confident.

When making tapes, the option of having music playing softly in the background can seem an attractive proposition but I have moved away from this. My attitude to making tapes is that I wish, not so much to produce a commercially viable product, as to provide for my clients the best content of most benefit to them. A tape is purely therapeutic and specially formulated, first to relax through the use of an hypnotic induction, and then to deliver positive affirmations and suggestions to the subconscious during the relaxed state thus induced.

I remember clearly being informed by a client that she had not listened more than once to the tape which I had supplied to her, as she found the music annoying. My reply: "That's interesting: did you feel perhaps that you needed to be entertained?" Obviously there are other messages within the statement, but let us not get too embroiled!

Music, however, can provide a useful vehicle within which to embed subliminal messages, and the tapes which I supply have on one side exactly that utilization, the advantage being that the tape can then be listened to at any time without danger, as long as it is the subliminal side and not the therapy side that is playing whilst driving the car.

Subliminal messages embedded within music are effective in that they by-pass completely the critical analytical processes of the conscious mind and deliver, unaltered by perception, those messages to the subconscious. This negation of the conscious mind to rationalize the content is extremely effective, and provides a powerful medium for therapeutic change.

I have heard the term "brain-washing" used by some. Well, I do not wish to become embroiled in any argument. The active content contained in the messages will help provide those changes which are desirable for the client, so I fail to see where any cause for complaint can arise.

Tapes should always carry a specific warning regarding their use and, in particular, the side that carries an hypnotic induction should never be used whilst driving or operating machinery. The dangers are obvious to those who are aware, but perhaps, just perhaps, there may be someone who is not aware and who could end up wrapped around a motorway bridge pillar as a result, so we must warn clients. Personally, I do so both by way of written instructions on how to use the tape, and then verbally at the start, before the induction.

In recent years, the development of video technology and the fact that now most homes do have a video player has resulted in the introduction of therapeutic video programmes using strategies hitherto unavailable to therapists.

I have seen a number of these videos, some of them utter rubbish and some, well, they do have some merit. But I am mindful of the powerful therapeutic qualities that are found utilized in the medium of "psychovisual therapy". This system was developed by a young graphics designer who combined his skills in computers and video technology to produce a series of unique video programmes.

The first of these was simply named "Relaxation", and used a mixture of colours (chromotherapy) and changing shapes, combined with music and subliminal messages, literally to bombard the viewer with relaxation cues, so that a light trance would be induced.

"As a hypnoanalyst myself, I immediately recognized the potential in PsyV, not just as a technique for relaxation but as a valuable aid in therapy."   **Michael Carr-Jones, 1992**

The popularity of the first title soon resulted in other titles, and before too long a small library was available. "Stop Smoking" was produced with the co-operation of a number of experts in the fields of hypnotherapy, art and music. While the viewer watched the beautiful undulating shapes and colours, listening to the soothing relaxing music, a state of light hypnosis was induced and, whilst the viewer was relaxed and open to suggestion, the therapy content provided powerful positive messages to promote beneficial change and reduction of the desire to smoke.

The success rate of the use of this programme in conjunction with traditional hypnotherapy proved very encouraging. Of the group comprising the trial subjects, in excess of 90% were still not smoking after six months.

Originally I began "Stop Smoking" therapy by conducting a standard hypnotherapy session with my clients and then, following trance termination, would have them view the programme through in my office, before having them take the video home to continue the therapy. I was following the recommended format for using PsyV, but I soon began to question the order of march, and then elected to turn the whole thing about.

I proceed by carrying out the initial information-gathering exercise and then directly to having the client view the programme; after all, the video contained an hypnotic induction, and my task proved so much easier when the time came formally to induce eyes-closed hypnosis.

The client, having purchased a copy of the video, takes it home, with my instructions that it be viewed at least once a day for the next seven to ten days, then at regular intervals, and finally as and when the need arises.

My success rate has proved very good, and, while not being in a position to quote scientifically-derived figures, I would not feel too ambitious in my claim of around 90% success.

The psychovisual titles are now marketed in this country by Psychovisual Libraries of Poole in Dorset, the company formed some ten years ago by Michael Carr-Jones, himself a well-respected hypnotherapist in his own right.

The videos are not sold directly to the public, but through approved clinics and health professionals. Many medical facilities have used, to good effect, the range of titles available, recognizing their potential for providing a valuable aid in therapy. They gently create new and positive images to lift the self-esteem, forming new and beneficial *habit patterns when the new values and positive motivations are stored as the imagination is stimulated to create personal positivity, confidence and well-being, to be held in memory.*

It is a fact that the "Stop Smoking" PsyV programme is the only therapeutic video to have received the accolade of acceptance from the British Medical Association, in recognition of its value as a therapeutic medium. It has also received a prestigious B.L.A.T. award from the British Life Assurance Trust.

More information about Psychovisual Therapy can be obtained by writing to:-

Lifestyle Libraries,
PO Box 1193,
POOLE,
Dorset. BH14 8YT
United Kingdom.

Internet Address:- Psychovisual @ Compuserve. Com

Hypnosis In Entertainment

"There is, I know, a growing strength of feeling within the profession regarding the use of hypnosis for entertainment purposes. I am not alone in my misgivings at what can be a demeaning of something which is, after all, a proven, effective therapeutic tool.

"Many people will not seek out hypnosis as a therapeutic alternative as a result of having watched stage hypnotism, because they cannot even begin to comprehend how what they have seen in a night club show can be used clinically to help someone in distress.

"Colleagues of mine have pointed out that many people seek out hypnosis in therapy because of the stage hypnotist, but such people tend to believe that hypnotists have mysterious powers, and so they approach treatment unrealistically."

Michael Yapko, 1990.

There is a danger, of course, that the imagination, unfettered by the critical, analytical conscious mind, will allow emotions and images to be created which will be accepted in memory as if in actuality.

Certain sensations and effects can be suggested which are potentially dangerous: in the same way that the power of suggestion can be used to help someone to stop smoking or biting their nails, suggestions can also, if delivered in an untrained and irresponsible way, promote a behavioural or emotional response not intended.

For those who have undergone formal training, the phrase "symptom substitution" will go some way towards the emphasis I seek here. As a therapist, I am aware that when I facilitate the removal of a symptomatic response, I must take care to ensure that I have dealt with the causative event, to ensure that I have not just made way for another, equally detrimental, substitute symptomatic response.

When using "Parts Therapy", it always good practice to instruct the "part" which is responsible for the symptom to accept a new and more beneficial task, an implanted substitute, such as helping with confidence or in a particular circumstance.

There are so many incidents where harm is done when an untrained and, dare I say, irresponsible person begins to make fun, tinkering with the delicate intricacies of the human psyche.

I paid a lot of money for my car; it represents, to me, a major investment. When I take it for its regular servicing or for repair, I am content that the garage which I have used for many years is equipped with all the necessary tools, and that the technician who will tend to my pride and joy is properly trained and is qualified to do the work. I certainly would not entrust my car to an untrained and unqualified erk whose only tool was a rather large hammer.

It seems reasonable that, when dealing with something as complex as the human psyche, we should ensure that unqualified thrill-seekers are not let loose with nothing more than the "large hammer" which equates so well with an easily-learned ability to induce hypnosis in very susceptible people.

It is necessary to look very carefully at the use of hypnosis for entertainment purposes, for so many misconceptions can arise from what is seen to be some kind of controlling magic.

The first consideration has to be the subject and his/her susceptibility, and the second his/her state of mind and general state of health, including depressive tendencies, epilepsy and even psychotic tendencies etc., etc..

How on earth can a stage hypnotist have knowledge of these so important factors before he begins messing with their subconscious? It is imperative that he implement a considered means of carefully vetting his subjects.

Be warned: before hypnotising anyone, it is absolutely essential that the subject's personal history be investigated, for it is a fact that cases of damage levelled at stage hypnotists have invariably revealed that subject had problems before the event.

I myself have had the experience of having to help people whom I term "victims" of stage hypnosis, who have been traumatised by their experience. Without exception, they have proved to be people who had problems to begin with, and the experience of the stage show has served to heighten their insecurities and feelings of lack of control. They should never have got past a realistic vetting procedure.

Some clients express a real concern when beginning therapy regarding the all-important matter of control. Invariably, the source of their concern is their experience either as the "victim" or as a spectator at a stage show. It takes time to explain the reasoning behind the pronouncement that "Nobody can control the mind of another", and I would guess that many hours of my time have been wasted in this fruitless exercise. I would prefer that my time be utilised more effectively therapeutically.

Those who are selected by the stage hypnotist are the most susceptible that he can find, those who will perform to order. He does not want those who will provide a challenge to his "powers". Those he picks are, in the first instance volunteers, because they are not concerned with the fact that they will be made to look silly. They want to be the centre of attention, and are willing to subject themselves to the ridiculous suggestions which will be the content of the show.

If they were not willing to accept the suggestions of the hypnotist perhaps because the suggestions fell outside their normal moral perameters, or were dangerous - they would simply be shocked out of trance if in fact hypnotised and refuse to comply. The embarrassment that can result from a suggestion that someone perform sometimes lewd and even disgusting acts is real. It may just be that the young woman who begins to remove her clothing in line with a suggestion by the hypnotist is in fact acting out one of her fantasies.

The question as to whether or not she is acting within her normal moral constraints then does become somewhat difficult. Inhibitions are certainly affected within the trance state.

What a mind-bending thought, that you or I could in fact control the mind of another. Surely every hypnotist in the land with just a modicum of skill and knowledge would become extremely rich in a very short time, as bank managers emptied their vaults at a simple suggestion! The proposal is simply too ridiculous and not worthy of the time and concern that, sadly, it commands.

I am not opposed to stage hypnotism to such a degree as those who would like to see it banned; there are some performers who are extremely careful and do ensure that they do not cause any harm, by means of vetting those who volunteer to come up on stage. I would personally like to see strict, enforceable guidelines laid down so that every person calling himself a hypnotist should be licensed within stringent requirements as to qualification. I have no doubt that the debate will continue.

As a therapist, you will find yourself in the privileged position of being trusted by people who sometimes feel that they have no reason at all to extend their trust to anyone. I would suggest that you owe it to the profession, to those who will be your clients, and then to yourself, to be the best that you can, keeping an open mind.

We cannot both judge others from within the constraints of our own experience and then allow them to be responsible for their own life. We are not advisors and how can we be, when the advice given usually begins with "If I were you..."?

We are not that person, and we never can stand in their shoes, or experience in the way that they do, or feel their pain. The most valuable thing we can offer is the help that they require to help themselves better understand, and restore in them the faith that they need in their own abilities and capacities to make the judge-ments and decisions which are right for them; to help them gain that confidence which tells us all that it really is okay to be who we are.

Bibliography

Andreas, Steve & Andreas, Connirae:
   Change Your Mind And Keep The Change.
   Real People Press, 1987

Anson, Barrie:
   Holism Homeopathy Healing And The Hereafter.
   Wessex Aquarian, 1992

Bandler, Richard:
   Using Your Brain ... For A Change.
   Real People Press, 1985

Bandler, Richard & Grinder, John:
   Trance-formations: Neuro-Linguistic Programming and the Structure Of Hypnosis.
   Real People Press, 1981

Bandler, Richard & Grinder, John:
   Patterns Of The Hypnotic Techniques Of Milton H. Erickson M.D..
   Metamorphous Press, 1975

Charlesworth, Edward A. & Nathan, Ronald G.:
   Stress Management: A Comprehensive Guide To Wellness.
   Ballantine Books, 1985

Charlesworth, Edward A. & Nathan, Ronald G.:
   Stress Management: A Conceptual And Procedural Guide.
   Biobehavioral Books, 1980

Citrenbaum, Charles M., King, Mark E. & Cohen, William A.:
   Modern Clinical Hypnosis for Habit Control.
   W W Norton & Company, 1985

Dilts, Robert:
   Changing Belief Systems With NLP.
   Meta Publications, 1984

Dilts, Robert, Grinder, John, Bandler, Richard & DeLozier, Judith:
   Neuro-Linguistic Programming Volume I: The Study Of The Structure Of Submodalities.
   Meta Publications, 1980

Edgette, John H. & Edgette, Janet Sasson:
   The Handbook Of Hypnotic Phenomena In Psychotherapy/
   Brunner/Mazel Inc.,1995

Elman, Dave:
   Hypnotherapy.
   Westwood Publishing Company, 1964

Erickson, Milton H. & Rossi, Ernest L.:
   Hypnotherapy: An Exploratory Casebook.
   Irvington Publishers Inc.,1979

Gibson, H. B. & Heap, Michael :
   Hypnosis In Therapy.
   Lawrence Erlbaum Associates Inc., 1997

Hammond, D. Corydon (Editor):
   Handbook Of Hypnotic Suggestion And Metaphor.
   W W Norton & Company, 1990

Havens, Ronald A. (Editor):
   *The Wisdom Of Milton H. Erickson: Volume I, Hypnosis &
   Hypnotherapy.*
   Irvington Publishers Inc., 1996

Havens, Ronald A. (Editor):
   *The Wisdom Of Milton H. Erickson: Volume II, Human Behavior
   & Psychotherapy.*
   Irvington Publishers Inc., 1996

Havens, Ronald A. & Walters, Catherine:
   *Hypnotherapy   Scripts: A   Neo-Erickson   Approach   To
   Persuasive Healing.*
   Brunner/Mazel Inc., 1989

Hilgard, Ernest R. & Hilgard, Josephine R.:
   Hypnosis In The Relief Of Pain.
   Brunner/Mazel Inc.,1994

Kennedy, Eugene & Charles, Sarah:
   On Becoming A Counselor.
   Crossroad Publishing Company, 1977

Kopp, Richard R.:
   Metaphor Therapy: Using Client-Generated Metaphors In Psychotherapy.
   Brunner/Mazel Inc.,1995

Knight, Brian & Carr-Jones, Michael:
   Love, Sex & Hypnosis.
   Chessnut Press,1992

Lankton, Stephen R. & Lankton, Carol H.:
   The Answer Within: A Clinical Framework Of Ericksonian Therapy.
   Brunner/Mazel Inc., 1983

Mills, Joyce C. & Crowley, Richard J.:
   Therapeutic Metaphors For Children And The Child Within.
   Brunner/Mazel Inc.,1986

O'Hanlon, William Hudson:
   Taproots: Underlying Principles Of Milton Erickson's Therapy And Hypnosis.
   W W Norton & Company, 1987

Orbach, Susie:
   Fat is a Feminist Issue.
   Berkeley Publishing Group, 1987

Tebbetts, Charles:
   Self Hypnosis And Other Mind-Expanding Techniques.
   Westwwod Publishing Company Inc., 1987

Waxman, David:
   Hartland's Medical And Dental Hypnosis (Third Edition).
   Bailliere Tindall1995

Yapko, Michael:
   Trancework: An Introduction To The Practice Of Clinical Hypnosis.
   Brunner/Mazel Inc., 1990

Videotape acknowledgments:

Hypnotism Training Film # 50 .... Gil Boyne 1991

Six Step Reframing .... Connirae Andreas 1992

The Swish Pattern .... Steve & Connirae Andreas 1986

Hypnotic Inductions .... Richard Bandler 1987